WOLVES UNSEEN

A THEOLOGICAL EXCAVATION OF CHRISTIANITY, CULTS, AND IDEOLOGIES

BOOK THREE

By Tekoa Manning

www.manningthegatepublishing.com

Also By Tekoa Manning

Walter: The Homeless Man, a novel

Polishing Jade, a novel

Thirsting for Water, a devotional

Jumping for Joy in the Midst of Sorrow, a devotional

The Spirit of Leviathan, Jezebel, and Athaliah, a teaching book.

Emmitt's Dinosaur, a children's book.

Unmasking the Unseen Book Series

Satan Unmasked, Book One

Spirits Unveiled, Book Two

Wolves Unseen, Book Three

King Revealed, Book Four

ISBN-13: 978-1-961773-05-9 (Manning the Gate Publishing LLC)

Wolves Unseen: Book Three Copyright © 2023 by Tekoa Manning

Unmasking the Unseen Series

Editor – Jo Fouts Zausch

Narrator – Lynn Brunk

Cover by Lynette Marie Smith
Graphic Design & Marketing

Picture on Cover by jimkruger

CONTENTS

INTRODUCTION

I surmise that I am in 4th or 5th grade. It is time for bed, but like most nights, I did not want to sleep; I wanted to read. I loved reading early on and had many books, but that night I longed to read my Bible. It was an adult King James Bible my mother purchased for me. I turn my bedside table lamp on and soon hear my mother coming down the hallway, standing outside my door. "Tekoa, it's time for bed, you have school in the morning—lights out." I tell her "Okay," and then I wait to hear the click of her bedroom door shut. My dad was usually in bed first because he got up at 4:30 in the morning for work—a dark early hour. I grab my Bible, lay on the floor on my rug, and open the book randomly. It lands on I Chronicles 1: "Adam, Seth, Enosh, Cainan, Mahalalel, Jared, Enoch, Methuselah, Lamech, Noah, Shem, Ham, and Japheth. The sons of Japheth were Gomer, Magog, Madai. . ." (I Chronicles 1:1-5, BSB). My dad opens the door as I try to utter the names and make out what the chapter is about.

He said, "I saw your light was still on. What are you doing down there on the floor, Tekoa?"

"Dad, I'm trying to read my Bible, but it's so hard."

And don't you know, my father actually got down on the floor with me and started reading! He read the whole first chapter of I Chronicles from Adam to the families of Ishmael and the families of Isaac–all the way to Father Abraham. After finishing the chapter, he looked at me and chuckled, and said, "No wonder it was so hard to understand. You were trying to read the begats–genealogy from Adam to Abram."

I have never forgotten this moment in my life. Some experiences change us. At that moment, I thought, wow, every name of every person in the Bible is significant. My young mind meditated on a God who created the animals, the trees, and flowers and formed life in the womb. And if this God had given us a Book that spoke of His power and characteristics, I wanted to read all of it. I wanted to read of the men and women who had made it inside the pages of His Book. Later in life, I realized the Bible was a canon and that the people of "The Book" had no book.

In Sunday school, I usually took first place when a prize was to be given for memorization or a biblical quiz. By age 10, I had memorized Proverbs chapter one, the Lord's Prayer, Psalms 23, and countless scriptures from the New Testament.

As I grew older, after experiencing much pain, abuse, and divorce, I still read the Bible daily. When I say I read the Bible, I don't mean I flipped through or started in the Book of John–I actually read it through and through. I don't say this with pride. I was raised by a mother and father who read the Bible repeatedly. I was studying the Torah (First Five Books of Moses) diligently before I knew what the word Torah meant.

Later, after my mother became sick with Parkinson's, she began following a healing evangelist. My dad took her to his conferences a few times, and she stood in line to get a touch from the Lord in hopes of being healed, but I detected something had a taint in the anointing. I began studying Satan, sickness, demons, and angels. I became engrossed with the prophets. I felt connected to them and the authority they used to expose the wolves in sheep's clothing.

Fast forward to my late 30s. One night, in the middle of the night, after being sexually assaulted years before and using alcohol as a Band-Aid, I was awakened by a Voice that sounded like all the waters in the ocean. The Voice reverberated through my being. The voice spoke five words, "*Get your house in order.*" I catapulted up out of the bed in fear. I went to my bedroom window, looked up at the moon, and thought, is the same God who hung the moon in the heavens speaking to me? I knew my life was out of order. Everything in it was out of order. After some time and prayer, I lay back down and received a download of the Book of Genesis (*Bereshit*) in Hebrew, Chapter One, being read to me inside my spirit:

> In the beginning Elohim created the heavens and the earth. And the earth came to be formless and empty, and darkness was on the face of the deep. And the Spirit of Elohim was moving on the face of the waters. And Elohim

said, "Let light come to be," and light came to be. And Elohim saw the light, that it was good. And Elohim separated the light from the darkness. And Elohim called the light "day" and the darkness He called "night." And there came to be evening and there came to be morning, the first day.

—Genesis 1:1-5, TLV

After each day of creation was read, again I would hear the Voice, but this time it was not audible:

Tekoa, get your house in order. Do you not know that I am a God of order? Do you think I gave you your life just to throw it away?

Suddenly, I had a holy fear of this God I had been reading about my whole life but knew I had never known in this manner. During the next few days, I did not speak to anyone unless I had to, and I didn't dare share my experience for fear people would think I had gone mad. Daniel and the prophets had similar experiences where they were unable to talk or eat. It was surreal. Shortly after this experience, I started becoming sick and too fatigued to finish a shift at work. Finals were happening at college, and I had tests to take, but one morning I could not get out of bed and stand up without falling into the walls. I was slurring my speech. It felt like I had been hit with a sledgehammer over the head. After becoming sick with neurological issues, I wondered if I was supposed to get my house in order because this God who had spoken to me was going to take my life. Could this be why I had experienced this? One morning on my 40th birthday, I got out of bed, and my knees buckled under me, and I could not stand up. I crawled to a table where my Bible lay, grabbed hold of the chair, and sat down, bawling. I raised my hands to the heavens and said, "God are you taking my life?" I randomly opened my Bible, just like when I was a little girl on the bedroom floor. The first verse my eyes landed on said, "This sickness will not end in death. No, it is for the glory of God, so that the Son of God may be glorified through it" (John 11:4, BSB). I focused my eyes again and reread the passage. Finally, I decided although I felt like death, God had a bigger plan. I do not suggest the Bible is a magic 8-ball or something we can randomly open, but in that moment, I knew the Father was speaking to me, and as time passed, I began to heal.

The little girl whose father read the Bible to her years ago had come full circle. Today, I have more understanding concerning the words from John 11, and how Adonai has given me a gift to write for those who desire digging deeper and for those who long for intimacy. I know without my season of suffering there would have been no oil. The crushing of the olive brings oil, and the crushing of the flower, perfume. At times this pen is heavy and hard to carry, but the end result is healing for the Body. Through my fiction novels, *Polishing Jade* and *Walter the Homeless Man,* my readers found healing from trauma and forgiveness for those who had hurt them the most. Later, when deep sorrow filled my life, and some of the most horrific rejection from those close to me, I birthed *The Spirit of Leviathan, Jezebel, and Athaliah*, as well as *Jumping for Joy in the Midst of Sorrow*. Book Three of this Series, *Unmasking the Unseen*, has been as emotionally difficult to write as my adolescent self, attempting to enunciate the genealogy of Abram. Exposing wolves and false prophets is never an easy task, but it is needed. Paul called several false teachers out by name in his epistles.

Often, wolves among us escape unseen. To unzip a fleece garment, one must be open to recognizing the characteristics. A religious organization can have much truth and still be a covert cult with a dominant wolf in charge. If I were to ask you if you were being hypnotized or enamored by a wolf in a wool coat disguised as a humble leader, more than likely you would answer no. The prophet Elijah was sent to wake up a people who had become encased in idolatry under the reign of wicked king Ahab and his wife Jezebel. In I Kings 18 the prophet Elijah exposes a spiritual table. There is a holy table. The Shewbread Table in the tabernacle was adorned with unleavened bread representing the twelve tribes of Israel. It is called the Bread of the Face. At Adonai's table there is intimacy, worship, fellowship, and the breaking and eating of bread, His Holy Bread, the Word. The table with bread that never goes stale represents our Messiah Yeshua. However, we must not forget that Elijah describes another table that has food, and if God's chosen people were aware of His table—His Menorah, His power—why would they long to eat at Jezebel's table? Jezebel was married to Ahab by her father EthBaal, king and high priest of the Sidonians. Jezebel promoted the worship of Baal in Israel and she murdered the servants of God (I Kings 18:4). Elijah had enough of the people's idolatry:

> Now then, send and gather to me all Israel at Mount Carmel, together with the 450 prophets of Baal and the 400 prophets of Asherah who eat at Jezebel's table.
>
> –I Kings 18:19, TLV

This bears the question: What do false prophets eat, and how do they speak? And why would Gcd's chosen people, unaware of their own condition, be so entangled in false prophets? Remember, judgment starts at His House (I Peter 4:17), and those who think they are incapable of being led astray, think again:

> For false messiahs and false prophets will rise up and show great signs and wonders so as to lead astray, if possible, even the chosen. See, I have told you beforehand.
>
> –Matthew 24:24-25, TLV

If great signs and wonders follow Yeshua's disciples and the apostles, take heed, for great signs and wonders follow the false prophets as well. Even if their predictions come true and they perform miracles and/or if they lead the people to follow other gods, darkness, and idolatry, we are told not to listen to them:

Suppose a prophet or a dreamer of dreams rises up among you and gives you a sign or wonder, and the sign or wonder he spoke to you comes true, while saying, "Let's follow other gods"—that you have not known, and—"Let's serve them!" You must not listen to the words of that prophet or that dreamer of dreams—for *Adonai* your God is testing you, to find out whether you love *Adonai* your God with all your heart and with all your soul.

–Deuteronomy 13:2-4, TLV

In Book Three, *Wolves Unseen*, we will examine what Yeshua meant when he told His disciples to be as shrewd as a snake and as harmless as a dove. We will inspect the separation of goats from sheep and who these sheep and goats represent. Other topics include idolatry, witchcraft, magic and sorcery in the Bible, clandestine cults, women in leadership, tithing pertaining to the seven feasts listed in Leviticus 23 and the New Testament, as well as the roots of Christianity.

I am hopeful you are enjoying this Four-Part Series, *Unmasking the Unseen*. In Book One, *Satan Unmasked*, we looked at Satan with a more Hebraic lens, the history of Satan and how he has evolved. In Book Two, *Spirits Unveiled*, we delved into all things concerning angelic beings, demonic spirits, witchcraft, sorcery, and deliverance. In Book Three, *Wolves Unseen*, the wool of the wolves is pulled back, and their bone-crushing teeth are exposed.

In Book Four, *King Revealed*, we will look deeper into the identity of Yeshua, the true meaning of salvation, and the 3rd temple, the priesthood, and the Book of Ezekiel.

Ready, Set, Let's Go!

Chapter 1

CLANDESTINE CULTS

PART 1

Often, wolves among us escape unseen. To unzip a fleece garment, one must be open to recognizing the characteristics. A religious organization can have much truth and still be a covert cult with a dominant wolf in charge. If I were to ask you if you were being hypnotized or enamored by a wolf in a wool coat disguised as a humble leader, more than likely you would answer no. However, some are in the clutches of a cult right now but can find no way out. Some cults teach truths, but they are manipulative and controlling and long to receive accolades from men. They love to keep the people powerless. They use bribery, such as "If you do not want to be part of a community or congregation, that's fine, but we are commanded to gather together" or "They left us because they were never part of us," "Let us not neglect meeting together, as some have made a habit." quoting I John 2:19 and Hebrews 10:25 out of context.

They say things such as, "God told me to tell you" . . . or "a spiritual awakening is happening here." Cult leaders are marked by authoritarian, militant control over their followers masked by a false humility.

At times, the leaders point out others that they feel threaten their ministry. If the other leader has doctrines or teachings that contradict theirs and has plenty of followers or members, they most surely find them intimidating. In order to hold things together, they will use well thought out means of persuading their audience that they are the expert and others can lead them astray. If a person has struggled with co-dependency, just know that cults and co-dependency go hand in hand. Author Steve Smith, an author and teacher who holds a master's in theology has an enlightening article entitled *Broken Cisterns: Cultic Codependency* where Smith describes the major unhealthy issue in cults today as codependency, calling it the greatest relational bondage within cults. Smith states that in a codependent relationship a person uses that relationship to try to meet all three of a human being's fundamental needs: security, love, and significance. But the relationship is a broken cistern. It cannot hold water:

> Codependency is a relationship addiction, which means that it appears to meet basic psychological, emotional, and spiritual needs of those who practice it, making the pattern hard to break.

There are two sides to the relationship: the person who is dependent, and the codependent enabler who fails to draw proper boundaries and allows themselves to be exclusively needed by the other person. Why is codependency wrong? Because it attempts to make a god out of a person. The Bible has a name for this: idolatry. [1]

In clandestine cults, often when people leave, they lose their families, friendships, and spouses or are placed in danger. When they finally realize how they have been manipulated, controlled, and deceived, they will attempt to exit, but this plan of action is thwarted. They are told they will be out of covenant, community, or headed to hell and will not enter the Kingdom of Heaven. Once people start moving away from a toxic group such as this, they find that their so-called friends who are still encased have little or nothing to do with them. Such cultic institutions as these exist under every title. Cults want codependency, people to be dependent on them and obedient, and they know just how to word things to trap the weak and vulnerable.

We hear a word or term such as cult, and instantaneously we picture Charles Manson, David Koresh, or Jim Jones, but some leaders are more covert while others proclaim to be the Messiah. Multiple men have claimed to be the reincarnation of Jesus Christ (Messiah). And one of them was not a man but a woman named Ann Lee (1736–1784). She was the founder

---

[1] Broken Cisterns: Cultic Codependency (Part 1 of 2) | Liberty for Captives

of *The Shakers.* Lee's followers believed her when she proclaimed to be the female incarnation of Messiah:

> The Shakers were founded in England in 1770 by Ann Lee. In the 1760's, Lee joined a sect of Quakers called "Shaking Quakers." The Quakers were said to "shake" because they danced and spoke in tongues. Lee had become dissatisfied with the Anglican church, and this dissatisfaction was coupled with the fact that Lee and her husband had had four children, all of whom died in infancy. Following the death of her fourth child, Lee claimed to have had a vision from God in which it was explained to her that sexual intercourse was the root of all sin, and that to truly serve God, one must be celibate. [2]

Obviously, be fruitful and multiply according to Genesis 1:28 was thrown out the proverbial window by the Shakers. Living things grow and reproduce, dead things do not.

When studying the history of cults and cultic leaders, we often think, "I am not that gullible. I would never get entrenched in a cult," but I beg to differ. When presented with elated news concerning a new congregation or a popular social media group, add a charismatic pastor, rabbi, teacher, or healer who comes highly prized and esteemed by our peers or a family member, we can easily be swept up in their teaching style, philosophy, or what we may consider wisdom in an area we lack. We may be

---

[2] The Shakers (virginia.edu)

vulnerable, needing friendships, a community, or perhaps we were raised in a cult unbeknownst to us. There is a fine line between religious institutions and cults. When new revelation is presented, and knowledge is added with deeper Hebraic meanings, a person can be learning new and exciting information and still be in a cult with a controlling leader or leaders who are narcissistic, twisting the truth, or consumed with filling a football stadium full of sheep–their sheep.

Leaders come in multiple flavors and styles. Some are also politicians, combining religion and politics. Other leaders have much truth and are humble servants, but many long to keep the sheep from leaving their assembly because they believe that they are the only ones who can protect their sheep from the wolves. Still some leaders are focused on numbers and building their own kingdoms, but our Messiah found one woman at a well worthy of a day's journey. Church houses range from snake-handling Appalachian men to stoic priests, pastors, Messianic teachers, and rabbis. Some leaders have degrees in multiple areas of expertise. Others were faithful and promoted and given a title due to favor. Today any Joe Blow can order a certificate and become ordained for twenty-five dollars online. Sheep follow shepherds, and if the shepherd walks off a cliff, if not careful, the sheep will blindly land at the bottom of a ravine.

Wolves are mentioned throughout scripture. The Messiah told His followers that He was sending them out as sheep among wolves. "See, I send you out as sheep in the midst of wolves. Therefore, be wise as serpents and innocent as doves" (Matthew 10:16, ISR). This message is not one for the faint of heart.

What happens to sheep among a pack of wolves? What about two wolves? On June 3, 2022, 143 sheep were suffocated to death. *CBS Saturday Morning News* aired a story that happened in Idaho. An attack by two wolves panicked a flock of sheep and 143 died after they ran into a steep gully where they were crushed and suffocated. 3

Sometimes the sheep that fall off a steep cliff are human. Arnold Potter, a husband and father of the Latter-Day Saints movement, after traveling on a missionary trip proclaimed Christ entered his body. In 1872 Potter announced at a meeting of his church that the time had come for his ascent into heaven. Followed by his disciples, Potter rode a donkey to the edge of the bluffs, whereupon he leapt off the edge intending to "ascend" but instead fell to his death. His body was collected and buried by his followers. 4

Reading Arnold Potters' ascent off of a cliff screams mental illness. The *Latter-Day Saints*, or rather LDS/Mormon Church, is considered a cult to many. Still today, what started in 1830 by Joseph Smith, a man who proclaimed an angel named Moroni

---

3 143 sheep suffocate in pileup while fleeing two wolves in Idaho: "The wolves scared the hell out of' the flock - CBS News
4 Arnold Potter (1804-1872) | Familypedia | Fandom

showed him where gold plates were buried on a hill in the United States, now boasts over 16 million members. Repeat, 16 million members trust the accounts of Joseph Smith and Moroni. *The Book of Mormon*, translated by Joseph Smith and published in 1830, has sold over 150 million copies worldwide. From the horse's mouth, the Mormons openly admit that Joseph Smith, founder of the Mormon church, had as many as 40 wives. Some of those women were also married to friends of his. And one was only fourteen when she became Smith's wife. The history of Smith should cause men and women to run in the opposite direction, but if a person has never read the Bible through or studied it as a Berean (Acts 17:11), a person can be led astray. Author Matt Slick, from CARM, *Christian Apologetics and Research Ministry,* exposes the narcissism of Smith in his article *Smith boasted that he did more than Jesus to keep a church together,* quoting *History of the Church, vol. 6, Joseph Smith Testimony Against the Dissenters at Nauvoo.* Carefully read the words of Joseph Smith and hear the pride that drips from the teeth of the wolf's mouth:

1. "I have more to boast of than ever any man had. I am the only man that has ever been able to keep a whole church together since the days of Adam. A large majority of the whole have stood by me. Neither Paul, John, Peter, nor Jesus ever did it. I boast that no man ever did such a work as I. The followers of Jesus ran

away from Him; but the Latter-day Saints never ran away from me yet."

2. "We have imagined and supposed that God was God from all eternity. I will refute that idea, and take away the veil, so that you may see."

3. "I told the brethren that the Book of Mormon was the most correct of any book on earth." [5]

The Mormon Church didn't allow black elders until the 1950s because they taught that blackness was a curse from being a fallen angel in a former life.

When naming what Christianity calls the founding fathers and reformers of our faith, we find multiple men with deranged behaviors. In the 16th Century Reformation, many men stood up against the religious abuses of the Roman Catholic Church. Men such as Martin Luther and John Calvin come to mind, but no men are perfect, and many fighting against corruption had their own demons to conquer. Don't we all? *Israel's Global Embassy for Research–The Jerusalem Center for Public Affairs* is a leading independent research institute since 1976 and has multiple articles on the origins of Christian antisemitism. Hans Jansen, author of *The Historical Roots of the Anti-Israel Positions of Liberal Protestant Churches,* cites an example of antisemitism exhibited by Martin Luther:

---

[5] Joseph Smith boasted that he did more than Jesus | carm.org

Among the Protestants' founding fathers, Martin Luther was particularly anti-Semitic. His writings were precursors of twentieth-century National Socialist texts. Adolf Hitler, Joseph Goebbels, and Julius Streicher gladly quoted from Luther's works, even if he never recommended the physical destruction of the Jews. Luther did, however, advise burning synagogues in honor of God and Christianity, confiscating Jewish books, and expelling Jews from Christian countries. In 1985 the World Federation of Lutheran Churches distanced itself from these statements of Luther. [6]

Luther died in the 1500s. 1985 is a long time to wait to renounce such statements of hatred towards the Jewish people. On the flip side, we are thankful for Luther's teachings on salvation being a free gift from God. Luther caused men to question the Pope's soundness and the church's authority. The Catholic Church exploited many in the Middle Ages by selling indulgences. In the Roman Catholic Church an "indulgence" was a grant or get-out-of-jail free card issued by the Pope. The unrestricted sale of indulgences by pardoners was a widespread abuse during the later Middle Ages. Although, it was not supposed to be a means of salvation, or to spare one from hell it became a means taking money from the poor. Prosperity gospel—medieval kings would employ monks to pray for their

---

[6] The Historical Roots of the Anti-Israel Positions of Liberal Protestant Churches (jcpa.org)

soul after their death and build cathedrals as a way to guarantee salvation. Indulgences was a financial payment of penalty to absolve a person of past sins and release a person from purgatory after death.

Catholics and Protestants have been murdering each other since Martin Luther challenged the authority of the Pope in 1517. From the crusades to the Inquisition to the War of Religion and other wars, billions of people have died bloody deaths, all in the name of God or Christ (anti-Christ). All in the name of religion. We often look to Luther and Calvin as men who brought change, and of course, they did, but how much of our history, the history of Christianity, are we oblivious to? The protestants were murdering each other, too. John Bunyan, 17th century author and preacher, was locked in the tower of London for starting a home group, preaching on the streets, and refusing to be silenced. Bunyan wrote the *Pilgrim's Progress*:

> Bunyan began his work while in the Bedfordshire county prison for violations of the Conventicle Act of 1664, which prohibited the holding of religious services outside the auspices of the established Church of England. Early Bunyan scholars such as John Brown believed *The Pilgrim's Progress* was begun in Bunyan's second, shorter imprisonment for six months in 1675, but more recent scholars such as Roger Sharrock believe that it was begun during Bunyan's initial, more

lengthy imprisonment from 1660 to 1672 right after he had written his spiritual autobiography *Grace Abounding to the Chief of Sinners.* [7]

It was not just street preachers who were imprisoned or tortured for their faith; many well-known scientists have been murdered over their religious beliefs, too. One such man was Servetus. Servetus's longtime friend, John Calvin, may have caused freedom in some areas, but he was not wholly innocent concerning Michael Servetus's horrific death of roasting. Michael Servetus, known simply as Servetus, was a Spanish doctor, theologian, mapmaker, and humanist scholar, but that did not stop his so-called friend from having him burned to death. Servetus believed that the doctrine of the Trinity represented a pagan corruption introduced into the Christian faith via the Greek philosophers. Calvin wrote his friend, Farel, on February 13, 1546, and went on record as saying if Servetus comes to Geneva, he would not let him leave alive. Calvin was compared to a protestant pope with much authority. But why did John Calvin have a death wish for Michael Servetus?

> Servetus was a Spanish physician credited with discovering pulmonary circulation. He wrote a book, which outlined his discovery along with his ideas about reforming Christianity – it was deemed to be heretical. He escaped from Spain and the Catholic Inquisition but came

---

[7] The Pilgrim's Progress - Wikipedia

up against the Protestant Inquisition in Switzerland, who held him in equal disregard. Under orders from John Calvin, Servetus was arrested, tortured, and burned at the stake on the shores of Lake Geneva - copies of his book were accompanied for good measure. [8]

Although John Calvin was only partially to blame and requested a beheading of lesser cruelty, he was indeed on board with the death of Servetus, whom he had known for almost twenty years. The newfound Protestants were doing what they had learned from the Catholic Church, murdering anyone who got in their way—anyone who disagreed with their theology.

---

[8] Galileo to Turing: The Historical Persecution of Scientists | WIRED

Wolves Unseen: Book Three

CLANDESTINE CULTS
PART 2

The Roman Catholic Church dominated Europe in the Middle Ages. Like most organized crime families, the Roman Catholic Church was aware of other bosses rising and was keeping an eye on the matter. By the 11th century, it had firmly established the law that apostates should be burned alive. The massacres at the hands of the Catholic Church are astounding. Several historians have offered figures of 50 million people being murdered during the 4th century until the 19th century. Author Grattan Guinness, an Irish Protestant Christian preacher and evangelist, expounds on the workings of the Roman church in its insatiable quest to regain control of power in his work *Romanism and the Reformation:*

> The rule of Rome revived in a new form and was just as real under the popes of the 13th century as it had been under the Caesars of the 1st. It was just as oppressive, cruel and bloody under Innocent III (1198-1216) as it had been under Nero and Domitian. The reality was the same

though the forms had changed. The Caesars did not persecute the witnesses of Jesus more severely and bitterly than did the popes; Diocletian did not destroy the saints or oppose the gospel more than did the Inquisition of papal days. At the Lateran Council in 1513, after all the so-called *heretics* had been silenced by fire and sword, an orator, addressing the Pope, said, "The whole body of Christendom is now subject to one head, even to thee; no one now opposes, no one now objects." [9]

To Christians in the 21st century, most of the church's history sounds completely barbaric, narcissistic, and ruled by cruel kings and queens. The famous Bloody Mary is a name penned on Henry VIII's daughter. Historians say Mary Tudor earned the title of Bloody Mary because she burned almost 300 Protestants alive during her reign. *History* website offers a thorough article, *Was Bloody Mary Real?*

As queen, one of Mary's most urgent priorities was returning England to the Catholic Church. She married Philip II of Spain, quashed a Protestant rebellion, and reversed many of her father and half-brother's anti-Catholic policies. In 1555, she went one step further by reviving a law called *heretico comburendo*, which punished heretics by burning them at the stake. [10]

---

[9] The Catholic Inquisition: "A Medieval Holocaust!" (excatholicsforchrist.com)
[10] https://allthatsinteresting.com/bloody-mary#:~:

And how can we forget the Spanish Inquisition and the treatment of the Jewish people during the time of Henry III:

> During the reign of Henry III of Castile and Leon (1390–1406), Jews faced increased persecution and were pressured to convert to Christianity. Faced with the choice between baptism and death, the number of nominal converts to the Christian faith soon became very great. Many Jews were killed, and those who adopted Christian beliefs—the so called *conversos* (Spanish: "converted")—faced continued suspicion and prejudice. [11]

King Henry III, known as Henry the Pious, enforced a new law called the Statute of Jewry. He planned to isolate the Jews and discriminate against them. During this time, relationships between Christians and Jews in England were difficult. The Jewish people were wealthy and mostly tolerated by the upper classes due to their wealth and ability to lend money to those in positions of power. The King was said to have borrowed an embarrassing amount and was unable to pay. So, what does the king do? He burdened the Jewish people with heavy taxes they could not bear. Sadly, a small child's death gives the King more evil thoughts concerning God's people:

> On 27th August 1225, the body of nine-year-old Hugh was found at the bottom of a well in Lincoln. A friar, sadly, was the first to accuse the Jews of kidnapping little Hugh and

---

[11] Spanish Inquisition | Definition, History, & Facts | Britannica

ritually executing him, using his blood to make matzos for Passover. Emotions flared all over England and Henry saw a chance. He thought he would ride public opinion and have ninety Jews convicted for the double crime of kidnap and murder. He arrested them, had them tortured and locked up in the Tower of London. Eighteen of the Jews hanged themselves rather than risk the anger of a Christian courtroom. [12]

Thankfully many of the Roman Catholic Franciscans who had been studying the Jewish faith pleaded with the court to release the Jews, explaining that the crime could not have been perpetrated by them. The Franciscans explained that eating blood in any form is prohibited for Jews according to their Torah, and Passover takes place not in August but in March/April. Sadly, ignorance among God's people and the Bible, especially the Torah, has caused much harm to many. We are as the prophet Hosea stated, lacking knowledge:

> My people are destroyed for lack of knowledge. Because you have rejected knowledge, I will also reject you as My priests. Since you have forgotten the law (Torah) of your God, I will also forget your children.
>
> –Hosea 4:6, BSB

---

[12] Franciscans helping Jews in the England of Henry III | The Third Order, Society of St Francis (tssf.org.au)

Donald Yates's Book *"When Scotland was Jewish"* details how persecution in England caused the Jews in the English government to flee to Scotland. Perhaps the person that caused most of the damage and false doctrines concerning replacement theology is a man named Marcion:

> Marcion (AD 85-160) was the son of a Christian bishop and teacher in Rome. While information on his life is scant, we know he was a wealthy ship owner with excellent organizational skills.
>
> Around AD 140, Marcion arrived in Rome and made large financial donations to the church. Almost immediately, he used his newfound status in the church and began disseminating his heretical views. By the year AD 144, however, the Roman church excommunicated him and refunded his money to him.

Although Marcion was excommunicated and deemed a heretic, he still influences Christianity today. Due to his money and power, his doctrinal views reached the Mediterranean. What was Marcion's central teaching? He taught that the God of the Old Testament was an angry god who was cruel and jealous–A god who created the physical world and drowned the globe in a temper tantrum. According to Marcion, the Old Testament needed to be removed from the Bible because it depicted an angry God and other books that presented Jews in a favorable light. After all, according to Marcion, the Jews crucified Jesus.

Add Gnosticism (Greek for Gnosis/knowledge) and dualism (separation of mind and body), and you have a concoction for disaster. In the end, Marcion's canon included a version of Luke he had desecrated and also ten letters of the Apostle Paul. Author, pastor, and teacher Ryan Leasure delves into Marcion and his heresies in his teaching, *Marcion: The Notorious Heretic of the Early Church:*

> Because Marcion had gnostic leanings, he believed everything material was evil, including physical bodies. Thus, when it came to his view of Jesus, he denied the incarnation — the belief that Jesus really had a flesh-and-blood body. Nothing so pure, according to Marcion, could be mixed with something so vile as humanity. Instead, it only appeared that Jesus took on flesh. This view, known as Docetism (taken from the Greek word *dokeo* which means "to seem" or "to appear") was common among the Gnostics.
>
> Marcion flatly denies the physical birth narratives of Jesus, and, instead, argues that the divine Jesus came down to earth at the start of his ministry to save us from Elohim's wrath. Furthermore, because he wasn't truly human, Jesus never suffered and died on the cross. [13]

---

[13] Marcion: The Notorious Heretic of the Early Church - RYAN LEASURE

Wolves in sheep's clothing, false prophets, and cults are as old as time. Marcion was the first to suggest that the Old Testament was outdated and needed to be removed from the Bible. Marcion's theology was deemed unfit, but the seeds he planted are still with us. Later in history, Justin Martyr, an early Christian apologist and philosopher who opposed Marcion and Gnosticism, began to assert that the "Church" had replaced Israel and the new covenant of the Church made the covenant of the God of the Old Testament with the nation of Israel a thing of the past.

Continuing, Irenaeus was a Greek bishop and theologian who defended orthodox Christianity against the Gnostics in the 2nd century AD. Irenaeus shifted the foundation of the Old Testament by reinterpreting the prophecies of the Tanakh as though they applied to the Church which removed divine protection from the Jews. But it was not just Irenaeus who helped plant the seeds of Christianity. Today this tree is larger than the redwoods with roots deeper than the sea. William Kewson, author of *Israel My Glory* blogsite, quotes Irenaeus in *The Roots of Replacement Theology:*

> Irenaeus, writing around A.D. 180, said, "They who boast themselves as being the house of Jacob and the people of Israel are disinherited from the grace of God."

> Origen, the most prolific writer of the early church (c. A.D. 250), grounded his Replacement Theology in allegorical

interpretation. For instance, when explaining that Jesus was sent to the "lost sheep of the house of Israel" he argued that the lost sheep are not Jews who are "carnal" Israel, but Christians who are "heavenly" Israel. [14]

What a sad, sad, religion we have created with its thousands of sects full of division and doctrines of men, but before you flee your assembly, online group, or congregation unexpectedly, dig in and find out why you believe what you believe. Also, humble groups who might not have dug as deep as you have might be a better fit to gather with. At times it is not what extent of knowledge we think we have, but it is the compassion and the people who are of one heart and eager to spread love to a hurting world. It is often our pride and bitterness that are the soil and water for heresy. I would advise researching the things written in this book. Ask questions and further, ask yourself these questions:

1. Do you look to a leader as the Bereans, or are you enamored by leadership? (starstruck)
2. Do you feel the leader has knowledge, and without the knowledge or his or her authority, you could be led astray?
3. Have others who left the group or assembly been shunned or shamed from the pulpit or covertly?

---

[14] The Roots of Replacement Theology – Israel My Glory

4. Do you feel an overwhelming loyalty to the leadership and do not want to let them down, so you volunteer to your own hurt and the hurt of your family?

5. Has the assembly or group asked you to help bring in new converts or market the ministry like a business instead of being led by the Ruach (Holy Spirit)?

6. Do you have to pay a considerable amount to join the group? Do you need to pay to read their latest blog series, as well as tithes, offerings, or expensive monthly dues?

7. Do you feel you must obey the leadership even if it involves becoming a member and signing a declaration that you will not leave the fellowship?

8. Do the leaders say things like, "We teach the truth here!" Or "Plant a seed here, and you will be financially blessed. You can't outgive God!"

Charisma is in the eye of the beholder. A charismatic leader makes an insecure person feel important; those who lack self-worth, are depressed, or lonely can fall into this trap. Are you a fan or a groupie or do you feel loved and accepted? Honoring leadership without placing them on pedestals can be tricky for those who were raised by shaming parents and seek praise and approval from man.

The list above is only a starting point. Often cultish behavior in leadership is tied to narcissism, and gaslighting is used as a tool to make you think that you are the one who is living in denial and would be completely lost without the wise council of your leader. Continue to search out what you've been taught along the journey. Find a safe community where you can grow and bloom and draw closer to the Creator and His Son Yeshua in peace and shalom. The community may not look like the traditional way you were raised or what mainstream Christianity looks like today. You might not fit into any box, and that's okay. Neither did a woman at a well, or Ruth, or Queen Esther. Elijah and John the Baptist were considered strange men who boomed with authority and spent a lot of time in the wilderness. The Father sees you right where you are on the journey. Follow the leading of the Spirit.

In Book One, *Satan Unmasked*, we uncovered the evolution of Satan. In Book Two, *Spirits Unveiled*, we discovered how angelology and demonology changed in our Bible, and especially after the Jews were exiled to Babylon and were introduced to Hellenism. Now, we must dig deeper to uncover *Wolves Unseen*. Wolves have been here since creation and they serve a purpose in the ecosystem, but wolves unseen are predators, along with false prophets and covert narcissistic leadership. We need to bathe in the cleansing waters and drink from the wells of salvation.

Chapter 2

THE CHIEF CORNERSTONE

Today, the church is very similar to *The Godfather*–full of criminal activities. Many notorious Mafia crime families grew from the prohibition era and rose to power. Each family had a Mafia Boss who was untouchable. Each church has a "*capo di tutti capi*," meaning "Boss of all the Bosses." Think pope or pastor. The Catholic church deemed Peter as the first pope, but Peter was not infallible, without err–no man is. Peter was not the first pope or priest. When Yeshua looked at Peter and asked him, "Who do you say that I am?" Simon Peter responded:

> "You are the Messiah, the Son of the living God."

> *Yeshua* said to him, "Blessed are you Simon son of Jonah, because flesh and blood did not reveal this to you, but My Father who is in heaven! And I also tell you that you are Peter, and upon this rock I will build My community; and the gates of *Sheol* will not overpower it."

> –Matthew 16:16-18, TLV

Simon means "One who hears." Bar (son) of Jonah (dove). The name *Peter* in Greek is *petros*–a pebble or small stone. The word *stone* is Strong's Hebrew Concordance #68, *eben*. *Eben* means *a stone* but is derived from the parent root *ben* which is Strong's #1121. Ben means son, and sons are men who build the family. In the original Hebrew alphabet, *eben* was a pictograph displaying a germinating seed and a tent representing our houses in bodily form. We are little tents or temples filled with the Holy Spirit. The tent of meeting set up in the wilderness was no ordinary tent:

> Anyone inquiring of the Lord would go to the tent of meeting outside the camp. And whenever Moses went out to the tent, all the people rose and stood at the entrances to their tents, watching Moses until he entered the tent. As Moses went into the tent, the pillar of cloud would come down and stay at the entrance, while the Lord spoke with Moses. Whenever the people saw the pillar of cloud standing at the entrance to the tent, they all stood and worshiped, each at the entrance to their tent.
>
> –Exodus 33:7-10, NIV

Or do you not know that your body is the temple of the Holy Spirit *who is* in you, whom you have from God, and you are not your own?

–I Corinthian 6:19, NKJ

When we combine the seed with the tent/temple, the anointing is passed down to the succeeding generations, from the seed of Abraham, Isaac, and Jacob to the Messiah. Peter was commissioned to spread the Good News of the Messiah and germinate the seed of His Father's House. After Yeshua's resurrection, Peter would preach the Good News, and the gates of *Sheol* (death) would not triumph because Yeshua conquered death and the grave. Peter knew who the Chief Cornerstone was, and Peter compared us to living stones:

> As you come to Him, a living stone rejected by men but chosen by God and precious, you also, as living stones, are being built up as a spiritual house—a holy priesthood to offer up spiritual sacrifices acceptable to God through Messiah *Yeshua*. For it says in Scripture, "Behold, I lay in Zion a stone, a chosen, precious cornerstone. Whoever trusts in Him will never be put to shame.
>
> –I Peter 2:4-6, TLV

Psalms 127:1 warns that if the Father does not build the house, the people labor in vain. In architecture, a cornerstone is the first stone laid for a structure. All the other stones are set in reference to this stone–the first stone set during the building process. In his article, *Little Known Purpose of the Cornerstone,* Architect Bill Whitaker explains that the cornerstone was hollowed out, and important documents, books, or photographs were placed into a metal container inside the hollowed-out area of the cornerstone before it was put in place:

> In the past, buildings were designed and built in relation to certain astronomical points of the compass. Ancient cultures believed that the position of heavenly bodies regulated life, fortune, and success; therefore, cornerstones were commonly placed facing the Northeast because it was thought this location would bring harmony and prosperity to the building and its owners. The ancient civilizations often performed a ceremonial ritual when the cornerstone was placed. [15]

Many of the Pharisees, Scribes, and political leaders had rejected the Chief Cornerstone. In the Book of Acts, the leadership questioned Peter and John as to what authority they had to heal the sick and preach the good news of Yeshua Messiah. In Acts 4, Peter quotes Psalm 118 and Isaiah 28 concerning a rock of offense and the Chief Cornerstone:

> Let it be known to all of you and to all the people of Israel, that by the name of *Yeshua ha-Mashiach ha-Natzrati*— whom you had crucified, whom God raised from the dead—this one stands before you whole. This *Yeshua* is "the stone—rejected by you, the builders—that has become the chief cornerstone.' There is salvation in no

---

one else, for there is no other name under heaven given to mankind by which we must be saved!"

–Acts 4:10-12, TLV

Therefore, thus says *Adonai Elohim*: "Behold, I am laying in Zion a stone, a tested stone, a costly cornerstone, a firm foundation—whoever trusts will not flee in haste."

–Isaiah 28:16, TLV

Yeshua is the Chief Cornerstone. Our Messiah, Yeshua, did not come to start a church or a religion with one man in power. In the Book of Acts, Paul refers to those who keep the commandments as "Followers of the Way" (Acts 24:14). Yeshua said that He is the Way. The Holy One is not in favor of over 42,000 denominations or the many differences in Judaism and the Catholic Church. We are to be living stones, unified, mature, and knowledgeable of the Word of God. We are told to hide His Word in our hearts, likened to the cornerstones of the buildings, which had words hidden inside the containers. The Ark of the Covenant was a box that had His instructions inside covered by the mercy seat. Our Messiah is the Word. Our Messiah is merciful. Brad Scott of *WildBranch Ministry* has a wonderful teaching on the Chief Cornerstone and the Ark in his teaching *The Tabernacle: The Ark* where he describes the heart of the matter:

As it is with many translated words, the English word *ark* does not fully describe this piece of furniture. Perhaps to some it conjures up an image of Noah or Harrison Ford. To many it is simply a mysterious box or an irrelevant ritual of the dark, foggy, black and white past. In Hebrew, this word is *'aron*. We would think of it as a chest, for the verbal root of this word is *'arah* or *gathering*. In context here it will be the container or gathering place for the testimony or the word of God, to be eventually expressed in the tablets. *'Aron* is in the feminine gender and not by coincidence. The bearer of the "Word of God" is always in this gender, beginning with the seed of the woman in Bᵉre'shiyt (Genesis) 3:15. The Word of God is pictured as a child in a womb, to be protected, kept, and nurtured. Five chapters earlier YHVH had given His people His word, and now He is giving instructions for a container for His words. It will be a pattern designed to show us where He will dwell. As we will see, there is to be only one vessel in the heart of the sanctuary, the ark. [16]

The Ark represents God's living Word and Yeshua the Messiah. We are to be walking in our callings in the freedom of Yeshua, not a man-made hierarchy or rulership. How did we evolve over time and become a system with man-made rituals?

---

[16] https://www.wildbranch.org/teachings/lessons/lesson33.html

How do we get back to the dusty hillsides and fishing boats where Yeshua Messiah fed people and multiplied bread from heaven? If we don't know our history or how we evolved over time, it is difficult to have a paradigm shift. Author and Hebrew scholar, Dr. Skip Moen, in his article *Prophet, Priest, Rabbi*, expounds on how God's order has been restrained by official ordinations to establish rites, rituals, and rules which prevent the free hand of God in the world:

> The church preached morality in the place of freedom. It became necessary to replace the outpouring of the Spirit for preaching, prayer, biblical study, and the celebration of the eucharist according to well-established rites. It became necessary to set up some kind of order in the confusion by introducing liturgical prayers and reducing the place of free exposition of the Bible in favor of liturgies. The more ignorant the lower clergy were, the more necessary it was not to allow them to speak freely but to make them the officiants of a set cult created by others who had a better awareness of the faith and were trying to live in a stricter fashion. Morality and ritual are the great means of defense against the perversion of all order that resulted from the new entry of the masses into the church with no authenticity of faith. [17]

---

[17] Prophet, Priest, Rabbi | Hebrew Word Study | Skip Moen

Has the "church" been left with religion instead of a relationship that includes faithfulness? Have we left a living, breathing God for a book about Him that we fight and argue over? I am afraid the so called "church" has left the Messiah out of the equation for theology and dogma instead of true relationship with the Creator of all the earth. Dr. Richard C. Halverson, chaplain to the U.S. Senate, said it best:

> In the beginning, the "church" was a fellowship of men and women centering on the living Christ (Messiah). Then the church moved to Greece, where it became a philosophy. Then it moved to Rome, where it became an institution. Next it moved to Europe where it became a culture, and, finally, it moved to America where it became an enterprise.

Continuing with Peter: The Roman Catholic Church teaches that Yeshua Messiah established Peter as the first pope. In Matthew 16, Peter professed that Yeshua was the Messiah, the Son of the living Elohim. Later in the story, before a rooster crowed three times, Peter screams, *"I tell you, I don't know this man!"*

A side note:

A trumpet call, known as the "cockcrow," signaled the end of the 3rd and beginning of the 4th watch." (chickens and roosters were not permitted to be in Jerusalem)

When Yeshua told Peter he would deny him three times before the cock crowed, our Western minds envision a barnyard with a rooster belting out, cock a doodle doo. Cock's crow" is a technical term in Jewish law: kri'at hagever. It is a time of day before dawn that marks the end of nighttime. In the Temple precinct, there was a Temple crier who called out to begin the service. Everywhere else, the time would be verified by a cock crowing. Peter would have understood the timing of when he was to deny the Messiah, and Peter was warned to pray so that he would not fall into temptation.

In Matthew 16:18, when Yeshua said, "Upon this rock I will build my church," He meant *ekklesia/edah*—His kingdom on Earth. He was not talking about a fleshly man named Peter who denied Him three times or a building. Peter repented and was faithful to feed Yeshua's lambs. We, too, are capable of falling as Peter did, but my point is Peter is not the *capo di tutti capi*, The Rock. Peter was never the first pope. Peter was never sent to preach to the Gentiles. Peter was sent to the lost tribes. Both those who had never been in covenant, and those removed from covenant—the lost sheep of the House of Israel—who God had written a certificate of divorce and sent away (Jeremiah 3:8). Yeshua gives specific instructions to the twelve apostles in Matthew 10:

> These twelve Jesus sent out and commanded them, saying: "Do not go into the way of the Gentiles, and do not

35

enter a city of the Samaritans. But go rather to the lost sheep of the house of Israel. And as you go, preach, saying, 'The kingdom of heaven is at hand."

–Matthew 10:5-7, NKJ

And who does Peter write letters to?

Peter, an emissary of Messiah *Yeshua*, To the sojourners of the Diaspora in Pontus, Galatia, Cappadocia, Asia, and Bithynia—chosen according to the foreknowledge of God the Father, set apart by the *Ruach* for obedience and for sprinkling with the blood of *Yeshua* the Messiah: May grace and *shalom* be multiplied to you.

–I Peter 1:1-2, TLV

Peter writes to the sojourners—those who have been displaced. Yeshua tells them to spread the message to the lost sheep of the House of Israel first. The Jews were to be given the gospel first. And so they were. The apostles were helping prepare the hearts of the Gentiles so that they would have "good soil." Remember the seed that germinates—the seed of the Good News would take root and produce more. Paul stated, "I am not ashamed of the gospel of Christ, for it is the power of God to salvation for everyone who believes, for the Jew first and also for the Greek" (Romans 1:16, NKJ).

Author and teacher Herman Hoeh of *Nazarenes of the World Ministry* explains in detail the journey of each apostle in his article *Where Did The Twelve Apostles Go?* Hoah clarifies that Peter, in his capacity as chief apostle, made one trip to the Gentile Samaritans. But that was not to bring the gospel to them because Philip had already done that. Paul preached the gospel in Rome. Further, Paul never once mentions Peter in his epistle to the brethren in Rome:

> The order in which Peter, in verse one of his first epistle, named the provinces of Asia Minor — from east to west and back — clearly proves that the letter was sent from Babylon in the east, not Rome in the west. Rome did not become designated as "Modern Babylon" until Christ revealed it, much later, after Peter's death, in the book of Revelation, Chapter 17. Where did Peter spend most of his time after those first twelve years in Palestine?
>
> *Metapirastes*, the Greek historian, reports *that Peter was not only in these Western parts — the Western Mediterranean — but particularly that he was a long time"* — here we have Peter's main life work to the Lost Ten Tribes — *"a long time in Britain, where he converted many nations to the faith.* [18]

---

[18] WHERE DID THE TWELVE APOSTLES GO? – NAZARENE NOTES (nazarenesoftheworld.info)

Peter and Paul were used mightily to spread the Good News, but they were not popes, cardinals, or pastors. Paul did not walk down to the altar, say a prayer of salvation, and convert from Judaism to Christianity. He had no *King James Bible*. Paul's name was never changed from Saul, *Sha'ul* in Hebrew to Paul. Paul used his Roman name when preaching the Good News to the Gentiles, which was common practice at the time. *Paulos* also means *small* which may refer to countercultural humility.

There were no Jewish Christians in the apostle's days—no 12-step program. No Eucharist. No new baptism ritual. Why else would people be willing to be dunked underwater by a crazy prophet named John? The *mikvah* is a holy immersion which for God's people was familiar. No one sprinkled babies. No one fought over whether to baptize in the name of the Father, the Son, and the Holy Spirit, or in the Name of Yeshua. God's people also self-immersed as a sign of free will, unlike the forced conversions under the conquistadors and Spanish inquisition.

Like the stones of the temple that Yeshua prophesied would come down, not one of these doctrines of men can stand. All of it must come down. Yeshua gave us a formula and a way to follow Him—Keep the commandments, produce good fruit, and be fishers of men, but instead, we have made mere mortals into chief cornerstones, mob bosses, and wise guys. It is time for another excavation. How can Satan (Adversary) fall like lightning if we keep placing the adversary in authority by following men like the Pharisees who Yeshua corrected, rebuked, and called vipers? Not all the Pharisees were corrupt. We see Yeshua conversing with Nicodemus and others. The term *brood of vipers* is an *idiom* from the first century and was an insult used by others in ancient times. However, Yeshua and John the Immerser both called out the hypocrites, and they used the word *viper* to describe men who teach doctrines of men and keep people in bondage. Today we have men who keep God's people sitting on pews listening to false, powerless, motivational prosperity doctrines. The five-fold according to Ephesians 4 is mostly absent, but things are always evolving and changing. The question is how do we get back to the simplicity of the Messiah and the beatitudes?

Chapter 3

SATANISM, WITCHCRAFT, & WOLVES

PART 1

The 66 books of the Protestant Bible and the 73 Books of the Catholic Bible have a long history. The authors of our Bibles were Jewish. James, the brother of Jesus (Yeshua) was Jewish, and his name was Jacob (Yacov). The English name James is the identical name Jacobos, in Greek. The Book of Jude, also, written by Yeshua's brother, comes from Jacob's fourth son, Judah, or Yehuda, meaning "He will be praised" (Genesis 29:35). Yeshua our Messiah is from the tribe of Judah. The Book of Jude quotes the Tanakh (Old Testament/Jewish Bible) as well as other authors whose books are not in our Bibles.

The author of the Book of Jude is descriptive and paints a vivid picture of wolves in sheep's clothing, and Jude warns his brethren that they have *Wolves Unseen* gathering with them at their love feasts. Jude exposes these men and equates them to

Cain, Balaam, and Korah. The author's words cause alarm and introspection as the reader learns the fate of such men as these:

> These people are hidden rocky reefs at your love feasts— shamelessly feasting with you, tending only to themselves. They are waterless clouds, carried along by winds; fruitless trees in late autumn, doubly dead, uprooted; wild waves of the sea, foaming up their own shame; wandering stars, for whom the gloom of utter darkness has been reserved forever.

> –Jude 1:12-13, TLV

Jude compares these wolves in sheep's clothing to rocky reefs hidden from ships in the night. When the tide was high, and the reefs were out of view, the ships would plow into them and sink. Jude uses adjectives that describe men/women who break bread with those gathered, but he says they are clouds without water—liken to the fig tree Yeshua cursed in Mark 11. The clouds have the appearance of rain (Holy Spirit), but they are dry as the desert. The fig tree had green leaves but not a piece of fruit to be found.

When dissecting a wolf, we must know what to look for. In verse 16 of Jude, he makes a list of characteristics to describe these false prophets and wolves. Jude calls them discontented grumblers who spew arrogance. Jude says that these wolves flatter others for their advantage. II Timothy says that these schemers worm their way into the homes of weak-willed women who are always learning but never able to come to the knowledge of the truth (II Timothy 3:7). They are men/women who use praise as a weapon. Watch and listen. No lone wolves exist, but as few as two or three wolves can make up a pack. What do we know about wolves and how can we relate to the use of the word wolf as an adjective?

- A Wolf's jaw is so strong it can crush a bone rapidly.
- Wolfs are cunning.
- Wolves circle their prey.
- Sheep are a delightful meal for a wolf.
- Wolves mark their territory with feces and urine.
- Wolf gestation is around 65 days. Wolf pups are born both deaf and blind and weigh only one pound.
- Adolph Hitler (whose first name means "lead wolf") was fascinated by wolves and sometimes used "Herr Wolf" or "Conductor Wolf" as an alias. "Wolf's Gulch" (*Wolfsschlucht*), "Wolf's Lair" (*Wolfschanze*), and "Werewolf" (*Wehrwolf*) were Hitler's code names for various military headquarters. [19]

Hitler was a wolf. He was an anti-Christ. The Book of I John, written around 85-95 CE informs us that many antichrists have come:

---

[19] Fun Facts: Wolf - Fact Bud

> Little children, it is *the* last hour, and as you have heard
> that antichrist is coming, even now many antichrists have
> arisen, whereby we know that it is *the* last hour.

-I John 2:18, BSB

John knows it is the last hour. For each generation there seems to be a last hour. For the Jews during the Holocaust, it was the last hour. It was a time of Jacob's trouble (tribulation). For those during the Great Depression, it was the last hour. The last hour could be at any time. When men speak and do things the Messiah would never do or teach, they are antichrists. Anti means both against and counterfeit or replacement. The prosperity gospel is one example of this, but so is the tainting of the prophetic ministry. These so-called prophets make the true prophets look bad by making predictions and date settings for Yeshua's return.

Many of the prophetic ministries today flatter the ego. Psychics do a type of soul reading, but is it from Above? No! The men and women make promises concerning salvation, latter day revivals, false political election results, and all these types of words to line their pockets. These wolves tell their listeners what they want to hear and tickle their ears, and they gladly take money from people experiencing poverty and even widows and those in need. The wolves salivate and reinforce that if those sitting under their leadership will give and plant a seed (money), they will reap much wealth, and the Holy One will see their tears and heal their broken families.

However, the prosperity gospel was not the only movement growing and evolving in the 1980s and 1990s. The New Age movement was also escalating and gaining ground. I like to compare it to an inexperienced baker working under a 5-star Chef. The inexperienced baker has been given a perfect recipe for a cake, but the young one with the inflated ego decides to mix in other ingredients. Today the mixing goes unnoticed by many who are desensitized. God's people have become like the people Elijah confronted on Mount Carmel when he looked at them and said, "How long are you going to limp between two opinions?"

> So Ahab sent word to all the children of Israel and gathered the prophets together at Mount Carmel. Then Elijah approached all the people and said, "How long will you waver between two opinions? If *Adonai* is God, follow Him; but if Baal is, follow him." But the people did not answer him, not even a word.
>
> –I Kings 18:20-21, TLV

In Elijah's day, the people had a weak corrupt King named Ahab and his wife Jezebel, the murderess. Jezebel worshipped the goddess Asherah, worship which involved human and animal sacrifices, temple illicit sex, and debauchery. When the prophet Jehu is sent on a mission to kill Jezebel, King Ahab's son, Joram, asked him if he was coming in peace. The answer Jehu gives solidifies the power of Jezebel who had four hundred and fifty prophets of Baal and four hundred prophets of Asherah who ate at her table. Jehu answered, "What 'peace,' so long as your mother Jezebel's acts of prostitution and witchcraft are so many?" (II Kings 9:22, NASB).

One of the greatest forms of operating in witchcraft is found in the Book of Proverbs: "One who stirs up discord among brothers" (Proverbs 6:19, BSB). The need for defining witchcraft according to the Bible is essential. The Book of Samuel defines it in this manner: "For rebellion is as the sin of witchcraft, and stubbornness is as iniquity and idolatry" (I Samuel 15:23, KJV). Witchcraft is not a fairytale book depicting a picture of a woman with a black hat and a black cat flying on a broom during Halloween. No, that type of lunacy is what led to many innocent women being tortured and burned to death as well as grain blight, and ergotism, that caused hallucinations and killings of innocent women during the Salem witch trials. According to *Science Direct*, "Ergotism is a human disease that results from consumption of the ergot body in rye or other grains infected by a parasitic fungus of the genus *Claviceps*."

Europe in the mid-1400s became engrossed in "witch" madness and suspicions. Many so-called witches confessed to behaviors that were deemed wicked after being tortured extensively. Within a century, witch hunts were common and most of the accused were executed and burned to death. According to

History Today, single women, widows, and other women on the margins of society were especially targeted, as well as the mentally ill:

> Between the years 1500 and 1660, up to 80,000 suspected witches were put to death in Europe. Around 80 percent of them were women thought to be in cahoots with the Devil and filled with lust. Germany had the highest witchcraft execution rate, while Ireland had the lowest.
>
> The publication of "Malleus Maleficarum"—written by two well-respected German Dominicans in 1486—likely spurred witch mania to go viral. The book, usually translated as "The Hammer of Witches," was essentially a guide on how to identify, hunt and interrogate witches.
>
> "Malleus Maleficarum" labeled witchcraft as heresy, and quickly became the authority for Protestants and Catholics trying to flush out witches living among them. For more than 100 years, the book sold more copies of any other book in Europe except the Bible. [20]

Yes, it was the last hour for many during that time period in history.

The Oxford University Press features an article on magic in ancient Rome, *Magic In Greco-Roman Antiquity*. The article has a plethora of sources and photographs from archaeological finds,

---

[20] Witches: Real Origins, Hunts & Trials (history.com)

including amulets, magical gems, curse tablets, spells on papyrus and on strips or sheets of metal, inscriptions, symbols, drawings, paintings, small figurines and larger sculptures, etc. Magic and magicians were clearly a part of Egyptian life during Moses' day, and they are becoming more popular today:

> In Classical Greece of the sixth to fifth centuries BCE, Thessaly and Egypt had already been known as the prime sources of magical knowledge; but only Hellenistic syncretism produced the abundance of material now available. Within the Greco-Roman world magic formed to some extent a common tradition, yet at the same time each cultural region put its own stamp on it. The main traditions were those of Greek, Greco-Egyptian, Roman, Jewish, and Christian magic. While clearly distinguishable, these cultural contexts also overlapped to a considerable degree and produced a variety of syncretic forms. [21]

Judaism has mixed in witchcraft, and Christianity has mixed in witchcraft. The Bible is full of idols and symbols used for divination. Aaron had a brother-in-law named Nahshon (Exodus 6:23). This man and his name are interesting. *Nahshon* means *serpent*. Etymology: (*nahash*), *serpent, bronze,* or *oracle.* When Moses and Aaron appear before the Pharaoh, Aaron throws his

---

[21] Magic: Magic in Greco-Roman Antiquity | Encyclopedia.com

staff down, and it becomes a serpent. Mysteriously, the magicians and sorcerers are able to do the same:

> But Pharaoh called the wise men and sorcerers and magicians of Egypt, and they also did the same things by their magic arts. Each one threw down his staff, and it became a serpent. But Aaron's staff swallowed up the other staffs.
>
> −Exodus 7:11-12, BSB

The Bible is full of idols and mysteries. How does an axe head float? How does throwing a branch in the water cause a reaction? In II Kings, the prophet Elisha is endowed with power. He does not say a prayer. He does not ask God to bring forth the axe that fell into the Jordon River. Instead, he does something that appears as magical as Jacob taking branches and laying them in watering troughs at mating season to produce speckled and spotted animals:

> As one of them was cutting down a tree, the iron axe head fell into the water. "Oh, my master," he cried out, "it was borrowed!" "Where did it fall?" asked the man of God. And when he showed him the place, the man of God cut a stick, threw it there, and made the iron float. "Lift it out," he said, and the man reached out his hand and took it.
>
> −II Kings 6:5-7, BSB

Sometimes the snakes, dragons, and mystical language used by the authors of the Bible makes for wonder. What would it look like for a snake charmer to see his snake-like deception swallowed up by the prophets of old? Below is a list of things to ponder:

1. Abraham's father was an idol maker who sold them in the market. (Joshua 24:2).
2. Laban (Jacob's maternal uncle) had idols that Rachel took and hid. (Gen. 31:34).
3. After Jacob's sons wreak havoc on the men of Shechem for the sexual assault of their sister, we learn they have idols:

So Jacob told his household and all who were with him, "Get rid of the foreign gods that are among you. Purify yourselves and change your garments. Let us arise and go to Bethel. I will build an altar there to God, who answered me in my day of distress. He has been with me wherever I have gone." So they gave Jacob all their foreign gods and all their earrings, and Jacob buried them under the oak near Shechem.

–Genesis 35:2-4, BSB

Whether Joseph uses the divination cup is unclear, but he had one:

Then he commanded the one over his household saying, "Fill the men's sacks with as much food as they are able to carry and put money in the opening of each man's sack. Put my cup, the silver cup, in the opening of the sack of the youngest along with his grain money." So he did as Joseph told him.

When the morning dawned, the men were sent off, they and their donkeys. They left the city and did not get far, when Joseph said to the one over his household, "Get up, go after the men. When you catch up to them, say to them, "Why have you repaid evil for good? Isn't this the one from which my lord drinks? He even uses it especially to discern by divination. What you've done is evil!" So he caught up to them and spoke these words to them.

–Genesis 44:2-6, TLV

These cups and bowls were used as means of protection through incantations and spells. Dr. Alan J. Avery-Peck, in his article *Magic Bowls*, explains what these cups and bowls were used for and who used them:

The term "magic bowl" refers to a pottery bowl on which was written a magical formula used to drive away evil spirits or to invoke a deity's help in preserving and protecting individuals or a family.

During the Talmudic period, in roughly 300-600 C.E., such bowls were in common use in Babylonia by Christians, Mazdeans, Mandeans, and Jews. [22]

Besides diviner's cups, there was the casting of lots:

The Urim and Thummim (Heb. אוּרִים וְתֻמִּים) was a priestly device for obtaining oracles. On the high priest's ephod (an apron-like garment) lay a breastpiece (חֹשֶׁן) – a pouch inlaid with 12 precious stones engraved with the names of the 12 tribes of Israel – that held the Urim and Thummim (Ex. 28:15–30; Lev. 8:8). By means of the Urim, the priest inquired of YHWH. (*Jewish Encyclopedia*)

The lots were cast in the Newer Testament to replace Judas:

And they cast their lots, and the lot fell on Matthias. And he was numbered with the eleven apostles.

–Acts 1:26, BSB

The Bible mentions staffs that became snakes and staffs that swallowed snakes. Regardless of how its explained or explained away, many things in His Word, make you go "huh?" Witchcraft in all its elements has trickled into every area of religion and government. Deuteronomy 16 and 18, a most peculiar verse, states that directly after the laws concerning righteous judgment,

---

[22] https://www.myjewishlearning.com/article/magic-bowls/

not taking bribes or showing partiality, sorcery, casting spells, and divination are stated as detestable to God:

> Do not set up any wooden Asherah pole next to the altar you will build for the LORD your God, and do not set up for yourselves a sacred pillar, which the LORD your God hates.

> –Deuteronomy 16:21-22, BSB

> When you enter the land that the LORD your God is giving you, do not imitate the detestable ways of the nations there. Let no one be found among you who sacrifices his son or daughter in the fire, practices divination or conjury, interprets omens, practices sorcery, casts spells, consults a medium or spiritist, or inquires of the dead. For whoever does these things is detestable to the LORD.

> –Deuteronomy 18:9-12, BSB

The New Age movement has seen continuous growth, as well as other trends, such as the popularity of witches. The word *witch* is not a favorable word. Mostly, the popularity of such movements stems from women who no longer desire to be part of a religion which, in many cases, women are not allowed to speak or be in any authoritative position of power. Women today are gathering to celebrate the divine feminine of the goddesses. This movement may be, in all actuality, Asherah worship—the counterpart to the masculine energy of Baal that impregnated her with the rain. This rain is not the Holy Spirit rain.

The number of witches and Americans practicing Wicca religious rituals has increased dramatically since the 1960s. Author Deena Yellin from *USA Today* gives statistics that many parents may not be knowledgeable of in her article *'We're in the middle of a witch movement': Hip witchcraft is on the rise in the US:*

> Yellin quotes Helen Berger, "The numbers of Americans who identify with Wicca or paganism has risen from 134,000 in 2001 to nearly 2 million today, according to Helen Berger, a resident scholar at Brandeis University's Women's Studies Research Center, who has conducted extensive research and authored four books about witches and pagans.
>
> *TikTokers* who share their witchcraft tutorials and other magical content under the hashtag #witchtok have amassed more than 20 billion views. There are now podcasts, museum exhibits and an array of books and classes focused on witchcraft. [23]

If today's Christianity is going to reach the youth, they must become educated concerning the roots of Christianity. Today's younger generation is looking for something real. A faith that's tangible. A religion without dogmas and creeds. A religion that knows its identity and is not afraid to speak the truth in love. A

---

[23] Witches on the rise in US as TikTok, social media brings it mainstream (usatoday.com)

movement that knows the identity of their Messiah and the power of the *Ruach Hakodesh* (Holy Spirit). Many true prophets who cannot find a place in the church or their community often end up seeking out witchcraft—a New Age formula for their gifts.

There are many voices today fighting to be heard, and in the midst of all this there is a lot of confusion. This is not the time to sit on a pew and go home and shut the blinds. If women believers do not stand and begin to walk in humility and power, with the knowledge of the powerful women in the Bible who were judges, prophetesses, warriors, women who saved nations, women will have to answer to a Higher Court. Women today need to know they have worth. Remember, Jezebel has a table, and so does the Holy One. But if believers in Yeshua do not know the items on His table, how can they provoke those headed down a dark path to the way of salvation and the light of the world?

Satanism, Witchcraft, & Wolves
Part 2

Today, one of the fastest growing religions is satanism, and according to some, Satan worshippers are trending due to both the political climate and religion. Hollywood and celebrities in the music industry have made Satan into a cool rebel. Don't believe me? Watch the Grammy Awards for 2023. The main act was a pop star dressed as Satan with a host of demons seductively dancing around him. This is supposed to have a shock effect, but Ozzy Osbourne of *Black Sabbath*, Marilyn Manson, and Rob Zombie did that years ago, along with other death metal rock groups. This is an enticement for impressionable young adults who get sucked into the rebellious scene and support their music. These so-called popstars are wolves that are happy to take the vulnerable hurtful youths' money and accolades.

There are a few differences in the Church of Satan (Anton LaVey) and the Satanic Temple. The Church of Satan was started in the 1960s and gathered some famous attendees, including

Jane Mansfield. Anton wrote the first Satanic Bible which essentially promotes feeding your beastly nature as Anton refers to it and the ego. Their motto: If it feels good, do it. Anton's church in San Francisco did just that, including altars with orgies. Still, other satanic groups have sacrificed babies and done horrific unspeakable things to children and adults. A growing congregation in Massachusetts, The *Satanic Temple,* is spreading like wildfire, and they do not believe in Satan. I repeat, no red-horned devil. A person might be surprised by what the Satanic Temple believes:

1. (Educated leadership) Lucien Greaves co-founded *The Satanic Temple* in 2013 with fellow Harvard graduate Malcolm Jarry.

2. (Fastest growing religion in U.S.) In 2020 the Satanic Temple had over 200,000 members across the country. Today's numbers are well over 700,000.

3. According to the Temple's founders, they do not worship Satan.

4. According to Lucien, "It doesn't believe in anything supernatural, doesn't believe in an actual Satan or "magic" and instead has "seven tenets" that "encourage benevolence and empathy, reject tyrannical authority, advocate practical common sense, oppose injustice and undertake noble pursuits."

5. Lucien says, The Temple does get applicants wanting to join who want to do some genuine devil worshipping but

anyone wanting to sell their soul, get rich via spells or join the Illuminati are told to "look elsewhere." [24]

The organization is as much a theater of American satire as it is a place for believers. They worship themselves and decide for themselves what is good or evil, instead of letting the Creator. Co-founder Malcolm Jarry said. "The Temple, not to be confused with the Satanic Church, does not formally deify Satan as the personification of evil, but rather it sees him as a literary character, a necessary rebel while mocking traditional religion and calling out government's embrace of institutions like the Catholic Church." Still, rules without reason or relationship equal rebellion.

The Satanic Temple has 7 Tenets:

- One should strive to act with compassion and empathy toward all creatures in accordance with reason.

- The struggle for justice is an ongoing and necessary pursuit that should prevail over laws and institutions.

- One's body is inviolable, subject to one's own will alone.

- The freedoms of others should be respected, including the freedom to offend. To willfully and unjustly encroach upon the freedoms of another is to forgo one's own.

---

[24] Satanic Temple membership explodes as Americans reject politics & founder says Trump & Biden are scarier than the devil | The US Sun (the-sun.com)

- Beliefs should conform to one's best scientific understanding of the world. One should take care never to distort scientific facts to fit one's beliefs.

- People are fallible. If one makes a mistake, one should do one's best to rectify it and resolve any harm that might have been caused.

- Every tenet is a guiding principle designed to inspire nobility in action and thought. The spirit of compassion, wisdom, and justice should always prevail over the written or spoken word. [25]

The Satanic Temple, although operating with more educated leadership, they too have their own agenda and shock affects. As one friend stated, "Goodness without Godliness is self-perceived goodness which makes them believe they have goodness."

Witchcraft, Wiccan, and New Age is spreading and becoming the hip, cool, new way to be energized, clairvoyant, and healthy. Portions of Wiccan beliefs are also creeping into Christianity and the Messianic faiths. Sadly, many Satanists and Wiccans know more about the Creator's creation than Christians, and they certainly know more about the holidays Christians keep because they keep many of the same. One example is Easter. The Anglo-Saxons celebrated *Eostre*, the goddess of fertility. The main symbols were dying eggs because eggs represent fertility, or

---

[25] The Satanic Temple - About us - TST

women's ovulation cycle. Rabbits were also festive during the occasion, for rabbits are known to be fast breeders. Although those practicing New Age and such types of beliefs may indeed have knowledge in these areas, what they lack is the power of the true Spirit, the Holy Spirit (*Ruach HaKodesh*).

How can we the Body of Messiah show them love and spread His light? Pointing fingers and having a judgmental attitude is not going to provoke them to jealousy. Being religious and holier than thou is not going to strike up a good feeling conversation that draws them in. One area of attraction today is in holistic medicine. Possibly studying the books of wisdom and learning more about all the healing properties of oils and plants listed in Song of Songs, as well as throughout the Bible, might be a conversational piece. Most all doctors in the first century were mostly essential oils salesmen. If we truly believe the Father has refreshment for these tired, thirsty souls, we must offer mercy:

> Come to the waters. "Come, all you who are thirsty, come to the waters; and you without money, come, buy, and eat! Come, buy wine and milk without money and without cost!"
>
> –Isaiah 55:1, BSB

Yeshua had the same message for the weary woman at the well:

> Everyone who drinks this water will be thirsty again. But whoever drinks the water I give him will never thirst.

Indeed, the water I give him will become in him a fount of water springing up to eternal life." The woman said to Him, "Sir, give me this water so that I will not get thirsty and have to keep coming here to draw water."

–John 4:13-15, BSB

The world is searching for truth, freedom, something real and tangible. The world is searching for their identity that only comes through Him.

Although knowledge is increasing among God's people, many new book releases are joining Christianity and the occult, such as *How to Be a Christian Witch* and *Spell Crafting for the Christian Witch* by Valerie Love and T*he Path of a Christian Witch*, by Adelina Saint Clair. The authors of these books have educated themselves in many areas that the "church" has yet to examine, and because the Body of Messiah lacks wisdom, knowledge, and understanding of their faith, those like the authors above are gaining ground. The world has become hypnotized and distracted by the object they hold in their hands, cell phones, social media, news, TikTok, Twitter, Facebook and sex, violence, and idolatry. The Book of Jude sums up what Believers in Messiah should be doing during this time:

But you, loved ones, continue building yourselves up on your most holy faith, praying in the Ruach ha-Kodesh. Keep yourselves in the love of God, eagerly waiting for the mercy of our Lord Yeshua, the Messiah that leads to eternal life. And have mercy on those who are wavering— save them by snatching them out of the fire; but on others have mercy with fear—hating even the garment defiled by the flesh.

–Jude 1:20-23, TLV

All of us can sin and fall short of the glory of Adonai, but leadership should be held to higher standards, and the Bible says they will be judged more harshly. "Not many of you should become teachers, my brothers, knowing that we shall receive greater judgment" (James 3:1, ISR).

Sin and sinful behavior has been going on since the Garden. "There, for the grace of God, go I." However, things hidden in darkness need the marvelous light of Yeshua to become whole. Many times, we are not to turn a blind eye but expose the situation by using the Word as Yeshua did while being tempted by the adversary. Witchcraft, spells, tarot cards, and enchanters are enticing a younger generation, but if we walk in the light as Yeshua, we will draw all men to Him. The Body of Messiah should have more wisdom and understanding than the religions of the world.

Chapter 4

SHREWD SNAKES, HARMLESS DOVES

In Matthew 10, Yeshua tells his disciples he is sending them out as sheep among wolves. Then the Messiah tells His chosen ones to be as shrewd as snakes and harmless as doves. However, none of these descriptions are straightforward to unravel without returning to the Torah (The first five books of Moses). The dove was a sacrifice, a sweet-smelling aroma to Adonai:

> If his sacrifice to *Adonai* is a burnt offering of birds, then he should bring his offering of turtledoves or young pigeons. The *kohen* is to bring it to the altar, wring off its head, and burn it on the altar.
>
> The *kohen* should burn it upon the altar, on the wood that is on the fire. It is a burnt offering, made by fire—a soothing aroma to *Adonai*.
>
> —Leviticus 1:14-15, TLV

Doves are gentle and represent the Holy Spirit, but what of a serpent? In Genesis 3, we learn that Adonai created the serpent, and there is no suggestion that the serpent was once an angel who rebelled. "But the serpent was shrewder than any animal of the field that *Adonai Elohim* made" (Genesis 3:1, TLV).

How was the serpent shrewd or cunning? The serpent tricked Eve (Chavah) not by lying to her but by telling her the truth. In Book One of this Series, *Satan Unmasked*, the serpent in Genesis is thoroughly investigated:

The serpent said,

> "Did God really say, 'You must not eat from all the trees of the garden'?"

> The woman said to the serpent, "Of the fruit of the trees, we may eat. But of the fruit of the tree which is in the middle of the garden, God said, 'You must not eat of it and you must not touch it, or you will die.'"

> –Genesis 3:1-3, TLV

The woman changed the words God had given to Adam, or possibly Adam misled Eve and placed a protective fence around the commandment. She will be sure not to eat of it if she believes merely touching it brings death. Eve tells the serpent she is not allowed to touch the tree either. Genesis 2 gives the exact words Elohim said:

Then *Adonai Elohim* commanded the man saying, "From all the trees of the garden you are most welcome to eat. But of the Tree of the Knowledge of Good and Evil you must not eat. For when you eat from it, you most assuredly will die!"

–Genesis 2:16-17, TLV

After Eve tells the talking serpent that if she eats of the fruit she will die, he tells her you will not "surely" die:

The serpent said to the woman, "You most assuredly won't die! For God knows that when you eat of it, your eyes will be opened and you will be like God, knowing good and evil."

–Genesis 3:4-5, TLV

Jeff Benner, author and Hebrew scholar at *The Ancient Hebrew Research Center*, explains the conversation that occurred between Eve and the serpent with fascinating revelation in his YouTube Video titled *Did the Serpent in the Garden Lie to the Woman?* Below is a paraphrase of his recording:

The defining factor is "Knowing good and evil."

God or Elohim is one who knows good and evil.

The serpent did not lie here as God even says; the man has become like us, and He gives the definition of an Elohim,

One who knows good and evil. Again, look at the verses carefully that come next in the King James Version:

Then the Lord God said, "Behold, the man has become like one of Us, to know good and evil. And now, lest he put out his hand and take also of the tree of life, and eat, and live forever.

–Genesis 3:22, KJV

Even God said they would live forever. The serpent still has not lied.

In Genesis 2:17 it says, "but of the tree of the knowledge of good and evil you shall not eat, for in the day that you eat of it you shall surely die." But we have to look at this verse in the Hebrew. In Genesis 3:3, the woman repeats what God had said in 2:17, "God has said, 'You shall not eat it, nor shall you touch it, lest you die.'"

Now, Genesis 3:4 is where most get confused, "Then the serpent said to the woman, "You will not surely die." But this is not what is in the Hebrew text:

God said, "*Mot Tamut*" This can be translated as "You will surely die."

In Genesis 3:3 the woman says, *temutum.* "You must die." *Temutum* implies when you eat the fruit you will drop dead immediately. Eating the fruit caused death as they were kicked out of the garden, grew old, and then died, but the woman did not say what Elohim said.

The serpent says *Lo Mot Temutum*: "You must not surely die. As in drop dead right then. The serpent which we read was created by God did not lie but he did deceive the woman with the truth. 26

The serpent was shrewd. The snake was cunning. The dove is the opposite. The dove symbolizes love, peace, and hope, but the dove has other characteristics. A dove rested upon Yeshua after His baptism/mikvah:

> After being immersed, *Yeshua* rose up out of the water; and behold, the heavens were opened to Him, and He saw the *Ruach Elohim* descending like a dove and coming upon Him. And behold, a voice from the heavens said, "This is My Son, whom I love; with Him I am well pleased!"
>
> –Matthew 3:16-17, TLV

After the flood, we read of the dove in Genesis 8. Noah first sends a raven from the ark. Then, Noah sends a dove, but the dove finds no clean resting place for the soles of her feet. The omnivorous raven could feed on the dead, swollen carcasses prevalent after the flood, but not the dove. The raven is said to be one of the most intelligent birds. The raven is not only a logical

---

26 (92) Did the serpent in the garden lie to the woman? - YouTube

thinker but also a trickster that can outsmart a wolf. Ravens have been recorded mimicking the calls of wolves and foxes. *Animal Network* an educational animal directory stated, "Scientists believe that ravens may call foxes or wolves to a carcass that hasn't been 'opened,' because the ravens cannot get to the meat inside." [27]

The wolves tear apart the meat, and the ravens fly in and share a meal of meat.

Unlike the raven, the dove could not set its feet upon death or rotting flesh. After seven days more, Noah sends the dove out, and it returns with an olive leaf. The olive, too, is symbolic of the Holy Spirit as the menorah lamps were filled with freshly pressed olive oil. The anointing is representative of the crushing and pressing of the olives that bring the oil. But the olive branch, when held out to another, symbolizes peace and reconciliation. When meditating on snakes and doves, Yeshua, in drastic contrast, uses these symbols to warn his apostles to be wise as serpents and harmless as doves. What types of imagery does this statement evoke?

Author Thomas Watson of *Grace Gems Blogsite* gives three examples of men in the Bible who were both *Wise as Serpents and Harmless as Doves* in his article with the same title. Watson's illustrations are for God's people as instruction:

---

[27] Raven - Description, Habitat, Image, Diet, and Interesting Facts (animals.net)

Moses was a man *learned* in all the wisdom of the Egyptians, Acts 7:22. There was the *wisdom* of the serpent. And Moses was the *meekest* man alive. Numbers 12:3, "Now Moses was a very humble man, more humble than anyone else on the face of the earth." There was the *innocence* of the dove.

Daniel was an excellent person. Daniel 5:14, "Excellent *wisdom* is found in you." There was the prudence of the serpent. Daniel 6:4, "The administrators and princes began searching for some fault in the way Daniel was handling his affairs, but they couldn't find anything to criticize. He was faithful and honest and always responsible." Behold, here, the innocence of the dove.

Look at **Paul**, Acts 23:6, "When Paul realized that some members of the high council were Sadducees and some were Pharisees, so he shouted, 'Brothers, I am a Pharisee, as were all my ancestors!'" By this speech, Paul got all the Pharisees on his side. Here was the *wisdom* of the serpent; and verse 1, "I have always lived before God in all good conscience!" Here was the *innocence* of the dove. How lovely is this union of the *dove* and *serpent!* [28]

Watson paints a very vivid picture of being as wise as a serpent and harmless as a dove. Remember, the Messiah is sending out

---

[28] Wise as Serpents (gracegems.org)

his sheep (that's us) among wolves. Along with ravens, serpents represent wisdom in nearly every culture. Wisdom can be used for good or for evil. Unfortunately, the Church during the fundamentalist era shunned most forms of knowledge or wisdom unless it came from their own tradition or denomination. Daniel and Moses were both highly educated in their time in the secular world. "So Moses was educated in all the wisdom of the Egyptians and was powerful in speech and action" (Acts 7:22, BSB).

Animal Corner has an insightful description of wolf behaviors and lifestyles. And the message is eye opening concerning our walk, our seed, and bearing fruit. The alpha males mimic some of the false prophets, pastors, and leaders today:

> Alphas are usually the only wolves in the pack to breed, and they actively and sometimes aggressively prevent other adult wolves in the pack from breeding. If the other adults want to breed, they usually have to leave their pack and set up elsewhere. Wolf rank order within a pack is established and maintained through a series of *ritualized fights* and posturing best described *as ritual bluffing*. Wolves prefer psychological warfare to physical confrontations, meaning that high-ranking status is based

more on personality or attitude than on size or physical strength. [29]

This passage indicates that it does not matter who is the largest in the pack but rather who is the most aggressive and cunning. The dominating adult males prevent other adult males from breeding or producing fruit. And they do it by bullying. The characteristics in dominating male wolves are the same as with religious leaders pretending to be shepherds. These predators prevent the Body of Messiah from producing fruit, walking in their anointing, and callings.

Professor Zimmerman at Inland Norway University of Applied Science who studies wolves adds another layer of information regarding the alpha males and dominant wolves. The free wolves in their natural habitat do not act like the wolves in captivity. The dominant alpha wolves only exist in captivity. That's a total game changer to what most men and women are taught in the dating world and corporate world and even church leadership world. Also in lion packs, the lionesses do most of the hunting. But the male protects.

Author and researcher Will Hart from *Grunge, Static Media*, a multi-platform publication reaching more than six million readers, peels back the layers in *It Turns Out Alpha Male Wolves*

---

[29] Wolves - Facts, Diet & Habitat Informaton (animalcorner.org)

Don't Actually Exist In The Wild. So where did the term Alpha Male originate?

The phrase dates back to the 1940s, when a researcher named Rudolph Schenkel wrote an article on wolves called *"Expressions Studies on Wolves,"* according to Gizmodo. The paper, which pulled from research on captive wolf packs, suggested that wolves lived in social structures dominated by an alpha male and an alpha female. These alphas could be unseated through conflict, but as long as they remained in charge, they determined how the other wolves behaved and dictated the structure of their groups.

Later, a paper by a scientist named David Mech promoted this term further, according to *Discover*. People were quick to get behind this depiction of wolves and even to infer that the alpha structure must apply to other social systems, too, including the social system of humans. But, in fact, further research has suggested that this is not the case. "As early as the 1990s, scientists discovered evidence that alpha wolves actually don't exist in the wild." [30]

An understanding of wolf packs became more accurate when scientists expanded their observations

---

[30] Wolf packs don't actually have alpha males and alpha females, the idea is based on a misunderstanding (sciencenorway.no)

beyond wolves in captivity to deep studies of wolves living in the wild. Groups of wolves in captivity do form competitive social structures with alpha male and females, but in the wild, wolf packs are actually made up of closely related animals: namely, a mother and father, and their offspring, according to *Science Norway*. [31]

How fascinating to learn that animals in their habitat are not aggressive to one another but walk in the role of their Creator. When captured and taken out of their environment, aggression and fighting for dominance becomes the norm. The Nazis did this is concentration camps. They made a hierarchy of opposing factions that constantly turned on or tried to rule over each other. Most militaries use these tactics with prisoners of war. The British also did it when carving up the Middle East -Ottoman Empire to make sure the tribes never banded together and stayed in perpetual strife like the denominations.

Yeshua said, "So if the Son sets you free, you will be free indeed!" (John 8:36, TLV). When the "church" holds the sheep hostage and gives them no freedom to flow and breathe in their habitat, confining them to a pew and bullying or conniving them, then the church leadership are acting like the Nicolaitan's (those who dominate the lay people in Greek) who Yeshua hated due to

---

[31] https://www.grunge.com/948744/it-turns-out-alpha-male-wolves-dont-actually-exist-in-the-wild/

their works (Rev. 2:6). We are heirs of a King and no longer held in bondage in Egypt.

In the natural world, wolves are part of the ecosystem and help redistribute the elk herds and other large animals like moose. Keeping the population down or redistributing the population of these larger animals causes vegetation to recover along rivers and streams. Everything Elohim created was for a purpose. Big bad wolves are part of children's fairy tales that teach lessons, but we adults can still lack discernment when the wolf is dressed in our grandmothers' garments. Remember, the wolves in sheep's clothing are likened to the adversary disguised as an angel of light. The wolf in *Little Red Riding Hood* was disguised as the girl's grandmother. The wolf acted as if he had Little Red Riding Hood's grandmother's gentle characteristics. The Holy Spirit is always written in female form. She is our "grand" Mother. In Hebrew, the word that describes the Holy Spirit is a feminine noun—*ruach*. It is Strong's Hebrew 7307—*ruach*: breath, wind, spirit.

In the fairy tale the grandmother is devoured. Wolves tend to swallow people whole like a cunning serpent, but there are no lone wolves. A wolf pack might trail a herd of elk for days looking for an animal that shows any sign of weakness. The wolves go after large prey. They are not running in a pack to catch a small fry. Wolves want to destroy leadership and especially the apostles and prophets. According to Yeshua, when a hired hand comes to look after the sheep, if he sees a wolf coming, he does not protect them:

> I am the Good Shepherd. The Good Shepherd lays down His life for the sheep. The hired worker is not the shepherd, and the sheep are not his own. He sees the wolf coming and abandons the sheep and flees. Then the wolf snatches and scatters the sheep. The man is only a hired hand and does not care about the sheep.
>
> —John 10:11-13, TLV

At other times, the prophet is the wolf:

> Watch out for false prophets, who come to you in sheep's clothing but inwardly are ravenous wolves. You will recognize them by their fruit. Grapes aren't gathered from thorn bushes or figs from thistles, are they? Even so, every good tree produces good fruit, but the rotten tree produces bad fruit.
>
> —Matthew 7:16-17, TLV

The apostle Paul gives us a well-defined list concerning good fruit and bad fruit:

> The acts of the flesh are obvious: sexual immorality, impurity, and debauchery; idolatry and sorcery (drug abuse); hatred, discord, jealousy, and rage; rivalries, divisions, factions, and envy; drunkenness, orgies and the

like. I warn you, as I did before, that those who practice such things will not inherit the kingdom of God.

But the fruit of the Spirit is love, joy, peace, patience, kindness, goodness, faithfulness, gentleness, and self-control. Against such things there is no law.

–Galatians 5:19-23, BSB

A wolf in sheep's clothing is not just about bad fruit or no fruit. If a person wants to undress a wolf wearing wool, the person must know the Word of Adonai and the characteristics of wolves. A lack of good fruit is part of the problem, but so is a tendency to despise any form of correction by leadership. Not everyone is a wolf, many are trying hard to bring knowledge, wisdom, and understanding so that the sheep are not enticed but strong and able to protect themselves from deception. The dangerous wolves have a taste for the spotlight, narcissistic tendencies, control, manipulation, and no compassion for the hurting. To deal with such people, we must be as wise as serpents and as harmless as doves.

Wolves Unseen: Book Three

Chapter 5

SHEEP AND GOATS

PART 1

Shepherds were protectors. They were carefully watching for a lion or a pack of wolves. Their flocks knew their voices and were in tune with their brave defenders. The greatest shepherd who ever walked the earth was Yeshua, the Messiah. He is the Good Shepherd, but one day, He will separate the sheep from the goats. The prophets mention the separation of sheep from goats numerous times:

> I will gather all the nations and bring them down to the Valley of Jehoshaphat. And I will enter into judgment with them there, on behalf of my people and my heritage Israel, because they have scattered them among the nations and have divided up my land, and have cast lots for my people, and have traded a boy for a prostitute, and have sold a girl for wine and have drunk it.
>
> –Joel 3:2-3, ESV

The name *Jehoshaphat* means the *Lord judges*. The valley of Jehoshaphat is the same place as the valley of Armageddon. *Armageddon* is a Greek word. It is Hebrew Strong's 717 "*har Megiddo*. Megiddo's geographical location ran along the southwestern edge of the Jezreel Valley just beyond the Mount Carmel ridge. We learn that the dogs will eat Jezebel in the field of Jezreel in II Kings 9. Author Anna Myatt from *Immanuel* blogsite gives a play-by-play of this valley and the battles fought there in her blog *What is the Valley of Armageddon?*

> The Battle of Megiddo is the first recorded battle on earth, taking place in the 15th century BC. It took place between Egyptian Pharoah Thutmose and Canaanite King Kadesh. From that battle on, history has played out in this valley. Jezebel was killed in the valley (2 Kings 9:10). King Josiah was killed in this valley (2 Chronicles 35:20-25). The Battle of Ain Julat between the Mongols and the Mamluks in 1260 AD. Napoleon Bonaparte defeated the Ottomans here in 1799. Even a battle of WW I was fought here between General Allenby and the Turks and Germans. In all, somewhere around 200 battles have taken place in this valley, making it arguably the bloodiest battlefield in history. [32]

---

[32] www.immanuel-tours.com/israel/what-is-the-valley-of-armageddon/

History tends to repeat itself. Jehoshaphat means "Jehovah Is Judge." During Jehoshaphat's reign, Adonai delivered Israel from the mingled forces of Ammon, Moab, and the mountainous region of Seir. God caused the enemy forces to become confused and to murder one another. Today, as Israel is surrounded by rockets and the slaughter and kidnappings of their people (10-7-2023), the Book of Joel comes to life. In Joel 3, the separation of sheep and goats is evident. Might this passage also involve the Holy One's chosen people, Israel, and the nations who have tried to destroy her? We are told of a future time when the Messiah will sit on His throne and separate the nations that tried to destroy His people and take their land:

> Yes, in those days and at that time, when I restore Judah and Jerusalem from captivity, I will gather all the nations and bring them down to the Valley of Jehoshaphat. There I will enter into judgment against them concerning My people, My inheritance, Israel, whom they have scattered among the nations as they divided up My land.

> –Joel 3:1-3, BSB

Physical Israel and Spiritual Israel are defining topics that concern the land of Israel and all Believers who have been engrafted in. The land of Israel is more than just real estate. Adam came from the land, the soil. The Creator breathed the breath of life into him, and he became a living being. Abraham was promised the land of Canaan. The Israelites were promised a land flowing with milk and honey. Ruth told Naomi "Your God will be my God." What God? The God of Israel. Ruth became Israel just as you and I and every blood bought believer does. After Ruth cries out to her mother-in-law, she leaves Moab and travels to the House of Bread, Israel. This is both a natural and spiritual excavation. Christianity did not replace Israel as some theologians teach. Psalm 83 gives a prophetic look at a future time before the Messiah returns and sits on His glorious throne. The crafty plans of the enemy is to usurp and seize the land and the promises of God:

> For behold, your enemies make an uproar; those who hate you have raised their heads. They lay crafty plans against your people; they consult together against your treasured ones. They say, "Come, let us wipe them out as a nation; let the name of Israel be remembered no more!"

> –Psalm 83:2-4, ESV

However crafty the plans and plots are to destroy Israel, the prophet Isaiah proclaims that no weapon formed against Israel will prosper. We wait for the day when Yeshua stands on the Mount of Olives and rescues His people and sets up His everlasting Kingdom. It is here that we enter the sheep/goat judgment.

We read in both the Old and New Testament that when the Messiah, Yeshua, returns for His Bride, He will sit on His glorious throne and separate the sheep from the goats. With careful attention to detail, in Matthew 7 and Matthew 24, Yeshua gives the characteristics of the goats and the sheep. The goats believe that they are born again and anointed servants of Yeshua. Before the unveiling of the differences between the sheep and goats listed by the Messiah, there are other details in the Torah and the prophets concerning this separation. The patriarch Jacob, who became Israel, also separated sheep and goats.

In the Book of Genesis, Jacob's father-in-law, Laban, changes his wages ten times, and Laban's sons speak horribly about Jacob's character:

> Now Jacob heard that Laban's sons were saying, "Jacob has taken away all that belonged to our father and built all this wealth at our father's expense." And Jacob saw from the countenance of Laban that his attitude toward him had changed.
>
> –Genesis 31:1-2, BSB

Jacob tells Leah and Rachel that it is time for them to leave. Jacob cannot stay in a place where he is being treated with such disgrace and taken advantage of. As Jacob confronts Rachel and Leah concerning their father's abusive behavior, he describes a dream given by Adonai to him concerning Laban, and it involves goats and sheep. Jacob tells Rachel and Leah that an angel of God spoke to him during a dream and proclaimed that he had served his father-in-law with all his strength, but that Laban has played tom foolery. Laban changed his salary ten times. Even so, God has not allowed Laban to harm him:

> Now it happened when the flocks were in heat that I [Jacob] lifted up my eyes and saw, in a dream, behold, the males going up to the flocks were striped, spotted and speckled. Then the angel of God said to me in the dream, "Jacob," and I said, "*Hineni {Here I am}.*" He said, "Lift up your eyes and see that all the males going up to the flocks are striped, spotted and speckled. For I have seen everything Laban has done to you. I am the God of Beth-El where you anointed a memorial stone, where you made a vow to Me. Get up now and leave this land, and return to the land of your relatives."
>
> –Genesis 31:10-13, TLV

Jacob received knowledge from above that has only come to light recently, *epigenetics*. Epigenetics is when the chromosome that contains the genes is altered in some way without affecting the DNA sequence (the genetic code) itself. That alteration is heritable and passed down. *Psychology Today* describes it as this, "Epigenetics is the study of how the environment and other factors can change the way that genes are expressed." [33] Jacob tells Laban that he will remove all the speckled and spotted sheep, all the brown lambs, and the spotted and speckled goats; and these will be his wages. Then Jacob uses epigenetics given to

---

[33] Epigenetics | Psychology Today

him by God and places the sheep and goats in front of the watering troughs outwitting Laban:

> Jacob took fresh white poplar, almond, and plane tree branches, peeled away white stripped sections on them, exposing the white of the branches. Then he set the branches he had peeled in front of the flocks in the drinking troughs and watering channels where the flocks come to drink. Since they were in heat when they came to drink, the flocks mated near the branches, and the flocks gave birth to striped, spotted and colorful ones.
>
> –Genesis 30:37-39, TLV

Jacob's story concerning Laban is also a metaphor for the Messiah's return and the sheep and goat judgment. Breaking this down, Jacob later wrestles with God and receives a new name, Israel, hence a nation and a people. Many nations have tried to destroy Israel and God's people. Again, Laban (Jacob's father-in-law) tried to destroy Jacob and not give him his worth. The name Laban means white. He swindled Jacob and treated him horribly. The etymology of the name *Laban* according to *Abarim Publications* is as follows:

> The verb לבן (*laben*) means to be or become white. Contrary to modern understandings of white as a symbol, in the Bible white either denotes a blank state (and thus emptiness or stupidity) or the state of greatest resistance to the absorption of light, which comes down to pride,

stubbornness and more stupidity. Hence leprosy, or the "white disease" signifies unwarranted pride and arrogance. Contrary to popular conception, black and white are both dark, but black things absorb light and become hot (or smart), whereas white things reflect light and stay cold (or stupid). [34]

Could Laban represent the goats and Jacob the sheep? Could this also represent nations? I believe so. The *Geophysical Institute* at the University of Alaska examines why white spotting is so common in domesticated animals, and yet so rare in wild animals:

If a spotted animal occurred in a domestic herd, it would normally mate and produce offspring carrying the spotting genes. Furthermore, the spotted animals would be relatively visible to herders and readily identifiable as domestic and might have been unconsciously favored for these reasons. (This would be particularly true of early herding dogs, which probably looked very much like wolves. A herding dog with white markings would be far less likely to be killed by a shepherd thinking he was defending an early flock than would one that looked just like a wolf.) [35]

---

[34] Laban | The amazing name Laban: meaning and etymology (abarim-publications.com)
[35] "Ringstreaked, Speckled, and Spotted" | Geophysical Institute (alaska.edu)

Notice, without the markings, a good sheep dog protecting the flock could be confused as a wolf. Those who are spared from destruction in the Book of Ezekiel are marked. We as Believers who keep His commandments are marked:

> And the glory of the God of Israel was gone up from the cherub, whereupon he was, to the threshold of the house. And he called to the man clothed with linen, which *had* the writer's inkhorn by his side; And the LORD said unto him, Go through the midst of the city, through the midst of Jerusalem, and set a mark upon the foreheads of the men that sigh and that cry for all the abominations that be done in the midst thereof.
>
> –Ezekiel 9:3-4, BSB

Also notice in Ezekiel 9, this is not the mark of the beasts, but a mark separating the righteous from the wicked—the sheep from the goats. A similar verse is used in the Book of Revelation:

> After this I saw four angels standing at the four corners of the earth, holding back its four winds so that no wind would blow on land or sea or on any tree. And I saw another angel ascending from the east, with the seal of the living God. And he called out in a loud voice to the four angels who had been given power to harm the land and the sea: "Do not harm the land or sea or trees until we have sealed the foreheads of the servants of our God."
>
> –Revelation 7:1-3, BSB

Not only do we see this mark or sign but there is also another marking listed among those who serve Elohim and keep His commandments, yes, we too are marked:

> The LORD spoke to Moses, saying, "But as for you, speak to the sons of Israel, saying, 'You shall surely observe My sabbaths; for this is a sign between Me and you throughout your generations, that you may know that I am the LORD who sanctifies you. Therefore you are to observe the sabbath, for it is holy to you."
>
> –Exodus 31:12-14, NASB

During the exodus from Egypt, God separated the sheep and goats. He also gave Israel a sign; it was the blood of a spotless lamb on their doorpost. The death angel passed over their houses and spared them because they had the mark or sign on their doors. Passover, like all the feast days, are signs between those marked and those not marked, between speckled and spotted and those who are not.

Yeshua will set on His Throne and separate the sheep from the goats, and in Matthew 25 He gives us the definition of what actions the sheep took and what actions the goats took. He describes their characteristics. The Goats call him Lord, but He tells them He never knew them. What a fearful place to be in! The sheep are described as blessed by His Father. These ones will inherit the kingdom. Why? He explains clearly: "I was hungry and you gave Me something to eat, I was thirsty and you gave Me something to drink, I was a stranger and you took Me in, I was naked and you clothed Me, I was sick and you looked after Me, I was in prison and you visited Me" (Matthew 25:35-36, BSB). Part Two Sheep and Goats will look further at sheep and goats and how they represent nations and both spiritual and natural Israel.

Wolves Unseen: Book Three

Sheep and Goats
Part 2

When separating items, we tend to place like kind with like kind. A rational person would not place an ice cube tray on a desk or paper clips in the refrigerator. People separate items and place them accordingly. If sheep and goats often graze together and both are worth roughly the same amount of money, why would the Messiah use this terminology? Yeshua separates plants. The wheat from the tares. Both plants look alike until they bear fruit. The wheat becomes heavy with fruit and humbly bows its head. The tares bear fruit but its bitter, toxic and inedible. Both plants look identical until maturity. The Messiah is often separating in the parables he tells. Wise virgins are separated from foolish virgins. The separation of sheep and goats has to do with a lack of humanity and care for the poor and those who are helpless.

In Matthew 25, Yeshua says that He is going to separate the sheep from the goats. Sheep keep their heads down, eating grass and clover, and they follow their shepherds. Goats are curious creatures, with stubborn horns, that eat everything, but perhaps one only looks at this by characterizing the differences between sheep and goats and not nations and leaders:

When the Son of Man comes in his glory, and all the angels with him, then he will sit on his glorious throne. Before him will be gathered all the nations, and he will separate people one from another as a shepherd separates the sheep from the goats.

–Matthew 25:31-32, ESV

Could people also represent nations? Jacob wrestles and becomes Israel, a nation. Jacob's mother, while pregnant with Esau, was told two nations resided in her belly. Laban mistreated Jacob and deceived him with trickery. He robbed him of his wages and did not give him Rachel (name meaning lamb) on his wedding night. Could Yeshua be referring to the nations and people who have treated His chosen people Israel wrong? Could Yeshua be referring to His Bride? Jacob like Yeshua was also denied His bride at first, so he ended up with two in a sense. Rachel, Israel the Apple of His Eye, and Leah, the Gentile Church. Rachel was beloved but Leah was more fruitful in diverse ways.

Yeshua is the one who will bring restoration to the fallen House of David, who was King over all of Israel. The Messiah will gather the lost Sheep of the House of Israel. The Messiah will gather His elect (Spiritual Israel) from the four corners of the earth. Gentiles, lost tribes, and those who have accepted the calling of the Messiah are "grafted into" the Commonwealth of

Israel. Ezekiel 34, explains more on the separation and how also sheep too will be separated from sheep:

> This is what the Lord GOD says to you, My flock: "I will judge between one sheep and another, between the rams and the goats. Is it not enough for you to feed on the good pasture? Must you also trample the rest of the pasture with your feet? Is it not enough for you to drink the clear waters? Must you also muddy the rest with your feet? Why must My flock feed on what your feet have trampled, and drink what your feet have muddied?"
>
> Therefore this is what the Lord GOD says to them: "Behold, I Myself will judge between the fat sheep and the lean sheep. Since you shove with flank and shoulder, butting all the weak ones with your horns until you have scattered them abroad, I will save My flock, and they will no longer be prey. I will judge between one sheep and another. I will appoint over them one shepherd, My servant David, and he will feed them. He will feed them and be their shepherd. I, the LORD, will be their God, and My servant David will be a prince among them. I, the LORD, have spoken."
>
> –Ezekiel 34:17-24, BSB

The passages from Matthew 25 and Ezekiel 34 point to a future time. In the Book of Matthew, the Messiah sits on His throne in the Millennial Kingdom. This is the King pronouncing judgment on the Goyim nations and the leaders of nations. Yeshua explains that those on His right are ushered into His Kingdom prepared for them from the foundation of the world. At the same time, those on His left are given some of the harshest words ever written: "Then he will say to those on his left, 'Depart from me, you cursed, into the eternal fire prepared for the devil and his angels" (Matthew 25:41, ESV). The right side of our bodies represents the stronger spiritual side, while the left side is referred to as the weaker fleshly side. Jacob blesses Ephraim by using his right hand (Gen. 48:14). A wise man's heart is said to be at his right hand and a fool's his left (Eccl. 10:2). Oaths were taken with the right hand raised. Signet rings were worn on the right hand (Jer. 22:24). The Queen stands at the right hand (Psalm 45:9). Yeshua sits at the Right hand of the Father (Romans 8:34).

In Matthew 25, Yeshua explains the differences between the sheep and the goats in a more spiritual context:

> Then the King will say to those on his right, "Come, you who are blessed by my Father, inherit the kingdom prepared for you from the foundation of the world. For I was hungry and you gave me food, I was thirsty and you gave me drink. I was a stranger and you welcomed me. I was naked and you clothed me, I was sick and you visited me. I was in prison and you came to me."
>
> –Matthew 25:34-36, ESV

The sheep heard the Master's voice and were obedient to take action and care for the hungry, thirsty, naked, sick, imprisoned, and strangers. The goats are given a harsh response. Those characterized as goats ask Yeshua a question. "Lord, when did we see you sick, hungry, thirsty, or in prison?" He tells them, "Truly, I say to you, as you did it to one of the least of these my brothers, you did it to me." (Matthew 25:40, ESV). Ironically, the goats see themselves as sheep and call the Messiah, Lord, Lord. The word *lord* is *adon*:

> The Hebrew word *adon* is one who has authority over another or, as it is usually translated, a "lord" and is used in the Bible for both men and God. However, from a Hebraic perspective, a "lord" is not one who simply rules over another but rather one who provides for and protects those under his charge. [36]

> —Jeff Benner, Ancient Hebrew Research

In Matthew 7, the people present different types of work they had done, such as laying hands on the sick and healing them. In Matthew 25, the driving message was on servanthood. The people in Matthew 7 equate their works to righteousness and name each action in an effort to come into the Kingdom. They profess to prophesy, cast out demons, and do mighty miracles. Yeshua harshly rebukes them. He tells them they have not kept His commandments. They were a *Torahless* people. In Matthew

---

[36] Hebrew Word Definition: Lord | AHRC (ancient-hebrew.org)

7, Yeshua tells the goats, "I never knew you; depart from me, you workers of lawlessness." Lawlessness has been translated in our English Bibles as law or lawlessness but this greatly errors in truth. Torah is not law. The word Torah means "Instructions for a blessed life." Hebrew Scholar Jeff Benner expounds on the true meaning of "law' versus Torah in his article at *Ancient Hebrew Research Center, What is Torah?*

> A Hebraic definition of *Torah* is "a set of Instructions, from a father to his children, violation of these instructions are disciplined in order to foster obedience and train his children." The purpose of a parents *Torah* is to teach and bring the children to maturity. If the *Torah* is violated out of disrespect or defiant disobedience, the child is punished. If the child desires to follow the instructions out of a loving obedience but falls short of the expectations, the child is commended for the effort and counseled on how to perform the instructions better the next time.
>
> Unlike *Torah*, law is a set of rules from a government and binding on a community. Violation of the rules require punishment. With this type of law, there is no room for teaching, either the law was broken with the penalty of punishment, or it was not broken. God, as our heavenly Father, gives his children his *Torah* in the same manner

as parents give their *Torah* to their children, not in the manner as a government does to its citizens. [37]

We walk in Adonai's light and wisdom when we keep the commandments. The Torah instructions were always to be written upon our hearts. The Book of Jeremiah makes that plain:

> But this is the covenant I will make with the house of Israel after those days, declares the LORD. I will put My law in their minds and inscribe it on their hearts. And I will be their God, and they will be My people. No longer will each man teach his neighbor or his brother, saying, 'Know the LORD,' because they will all know Me,
>
> from the least of them to the greatest, declares the LORD.
>
> For I will forgive their iniquities and will remember their sins no more.
>
> –Jeremiah 31:33-34, BSB

Not only were those mentioned in Matthew 7 workers of lawlessness, Yeshua tells the individuals who call Him Lord that He has never experienced intimacy with them, and although they assume He knows them in this manner, He does not:

> Not everyone who says to me, "Lord, Lord," will enter the kingdom of heaven, but the one who does the will of my Father who is in heaven. On that day many will say to me,

---

[37] What is Torah? | AHRC (ancient-hebrew.org)

"Lord, Lord, did we not prophesy in your name, and cast out demons in your name, and do many mighty works in your name?" And then will I declare to them, "I never knew you; depart from me, you workers of lawlessness."

–Matthew 7:21-23, ESV

The powerful words "I never knew you" convey intimacy liken unto a marriage bed. Only the High Priest could know what it was like to go into the Holy of Holies on the Day of Atonement. Those on the outside could read about what was going on in the most holy place, but they did not see or feel it. A bride is holy and set apart for her husband. They become one and know each other in a manner that is sacred. Those who proclaimed Messiah as their Lord were far from Him. What a scary place to be in when we do not know our condition.

During the sheep and goat judgment, Israel must not be left out as a central point of the parable. The "church" has been given a warning in Genesis not to curse the land or God's people, Israel. The Father tells Abraham, "I will bless those who bless you, And the one who curses you I will curse. And in you all the families of the earth will be blessed" (Genesis 12:3, NASB). Throughout history, the Jewish people have experienced hatred and unspeakable evils. Dr. Michael L. Brown elaborates more on this in his article *Why Have Jewish People Been So Hated?*

What, then, makes anti-Semitism such a unique hatred? First, it is the longest hatred of all time, dating back at least 2,300 years (and even longer if the book of Esther is included). As expressed by the Catholic scholar Edward Flannery, "Antisemitism is the longest and deepest hatred of human history. What other hatred has endured some twenty-three centuries and survived a genocide of 6,000,000 of its victims in its twenty-third century of existence only to find itself still intact and rich in potential for many years of life?" Today, Anti-Semitism is at its highest levels since immediately before the Holocaust, equaling, in fact, those pre-Holocaust levels. [38]

Continuing with Israel and God's chosen people, does not this extend to Abraham's other genetic children outside of the Jews and to the Holy One's children who have been engrafted into Israel? I believe so. In Romans 11, we are told that Believers in Messiah were wild olive shoots that were grafted in among the others and now share in the nourishing root of the olive tree. Isaiah 29 says that Israel will no longer be ashamed. The redeemer of Abraham and Abraham's seed will sanctify God's Holy Name, and those who go astray will come to understanding. Paul said, "I ask then, did God reject His people? Certainly not! I am an Israelite myself, a descendant of Abraham, from the tribe of Benjamin. God did not reject His people, whom He foreknew"

---

[38] Why Have Jewish People Been So Hated? | Ask Dr. Brown (askdrbrown.org)

(Romans 11:1-2, BSB). The Holy One is the God of all the earth and all the nations. There is only one YHWH.

The nations and people who have dehumanized God's chosen people will have to stand before the judgment seat. The Holy One made a distinction between sheep and goats when Moses came before Pharoah. "But the LORD will make a distinction between the livestock of Israel and the livestock of Egypt, so that nothing will die of all that belongs to the sons of Israel" (Exodus 9:4, NASB). Those who choose Yeshua and walk in His ways will never die.

A hidden layer to the sheep-goat judgment in Matthew 25 is found in the disciples' instruction for making disciples. When Yeshua sends out His disciples, He gives them instructions. The Messiah tells the Apostles that He has anointed them with great power, and then He names the same works the people proclaimed to do in Matthew 25: heal the sick, cast out demons, and prophesy. After this, Yeshua gives a strict warning:

> "Take nothing for the journey," He told them, "No staff, no bag, no bread, no money, no second tunic. Whatever house you enter, stay there until you leave that area. If anyone does not welcome you, shake the dust off your feet when you leave that town, as a testimony against them."
>
> –Luke 9:1-5, BSB

Remember, in the parable in Matthew 25:34-36 those who entered the Kingdom gave drink, fed, clothed, welcomed, and visited Yeshua in prison:

> Then the King will say to those on his right, "Come, you who are blessed by my Father, inherit the kingdom prepared for you from the foundation of the world. For I was hungry, and you gave me food, I was thirsty and you gave me drink, I was a stranger and you welcomed me, I was naked and you clothed me, I was sick and you visited me, I was in prison and you came to me."
>
> –Matthew 25:34-36, ESV

Matthew 25 is also connected to Yeshua's apostles, the men He was training to go forth with the Gospel. In Roman times those in prison had to be fed and clothed and provided with medical care by their families or visitors. Paul relied on this, and in his letters often requested Timothy and others to bring him a coat, his scrolls, and other items.

Unlike the men in training to be apostles, the goats were oblivious to Yeshua's called-out ones. They responded by listing their ability to prophesy, cast out demons, and do mighty works/miracles. They were as the Book of Jude described, "These men are discontented grumblers, following after their own lusts; their mouths spew arrogance; they flatter others for their own advantage" (Jude 1:16, BSB). Jude calls them dreamers who defile their bodies, reject authority, and slander glorious beings. They think they can command angelic hosts to do their bidding, and they prophesy lies. These arrogant types of works then, and now, often draw more attention to these types of people. Meanwhile, in Matthew 25, the true servants of Adonai were behind the scenes caring for those others did not deem fit for the kingdom.

In Matthew 25, Yeshua says that He will place the sheep on His right and the goats on His left. In Hebrew thought, the left side represents justice and is said to be the weaker side unless one is left-handed. The right side is related to mercy and is said to be more spiritual. Jacob blessed Joseph's sons, and his right hand was significant:

> When Joseph saw that his father had placed his right hand on Ephraim's head, he was displeased and took his father's hand to move it from Ephraim's head to Manasseh's. "Not so, my father!" Joseph said. "This one is the firstborn; put your right hand on his head." But his father refused. "I know, my son, I know!" he said. "He too shall become a people, and he too shall be great; nevertheless, his younger brother shall be greater than he, and his offspring shall become a multitude of nations."
>
> –Genesis 48:17-19, BSB

The Father's right-hand shatters our enemies:

> Your right hand, O LORD, glorious in power, your right hand, O LORD, shatters the enemy.

> –Exodus 15:6, ESV

The Father protects us with His Right Hand:

> For I, the LORD your God, hold your right hand; it is I who say to you, "Fear not, I am the one who helps you."

> –Isaiah 41:13, ESV

It is Messiah Yeshua who sits at the Father's right hand:

> "He exerted in Christ when He raised Him from the dead and seated Him at His right hand in the heavenly realms."

> –Ephesians 1:20, BSB

Our Messiah is the Good Shepherd, and His sheep know His voice. The goats believe they know Him intimately and can discern His voice, but obviously, in the parable, they did not, and the works they proclaimed to do in His name were false. When the Messiah sits on His glorious throne, He will separate goats from sheep. We must be introspective and ask ourselves if we are a sheep or a goat. What are we feeding on? Do we have horns that headbutt others and run off from the good shepherd? Do we have a mark and a sign on our right hand? Are we keeping His holy feasts or believing in our hearts that we are busy doing good works when in reality, He may not "know" us intimately. Judas kept the Feasts and Sabbath and Letter of the Torah as much or better as other first century Jews. Judas only wanted the parts of truth convenient to him. He wanted the Messiah which was true. But not the crucifixion–also truth. Adonai said He hated it when people went through the motions of the feasts. The Book of Amos has some of the harshest corrections in it. The Holy One says He cannot bear their festivals any longer:

> I hate, I despise your feasts! I cannot stand the stench of your solemn assemblies. Even though you offer Me burnt offerings and grain offerings, I will not accept them;
>
> for your peace offerings of fattened cattle I will have no regard. Take away from Me the noise of your songs!
>
> I will not listen to the music of your harps. But let justice roll on like a river, and righteousness like an ever-flowing stream.
>
> –Amos 5:21-24, BSB

God's people thought they were acting like sheep. They were keeping the Torah, and yet they were also worshipping the stars, other gods, and neglecting justice and mercy for the poor and the fatherless. When the prophets repented, they repented for the whole nation, the people of Israel. When the King of King's sits on His Throne, he will rule like no other. His judgments will be just for the nations and collective Israel, both those who were born into the Nation and those outside who were taught the Covenant and engrafted in to walk in the ways of the Messiah.

Chapter 6

WOMEN WITH AUTHORITY

Today's women are more aware of their inner beauty and strength. Christianity and the false doctrines taught in the assemblies concerning God's daughters have left many women wounded and exiting the church. Early Christianity, like Judaism before it, greatly elevated women from where they had been. Yeshua's ministry started with women and ended with women. When Mary visited Elizabeth, John the Baptist leaped in her womb. Elizabeth recognized that Mary, or Miriam in Hebrew, was pregnant with the Messiah. It was a woman who anointed the Messiah's head and a woman who anointed his feet. It was a woman Yeshua appeared to first after the resurrection.

CBE International, whose slogan is *Our Justice Issue is Women, and our Authority is the Bible* contains an academic article, titled *The Place of Women in First-century Synagogues: They were much more active in religious life than they are today,* offers much to glean from:

In the first century, women were the equals of men religiously and frequently visited the synagogue. This can easily be documented from literary sources. Here are just a few examples:

Judges 5:24 records Deborah's blessing of Jael — "most blessed of women in tents." The Targum's translation is: "Like one of the women who attend the houses of study she will be blessed," translating "tents" as "houses of study." "House of study" (in Hebrew, *bet midrash)* is an equivalent expression for "synagogue," since the "house of study" was usually connected with a synagogue, and studies took place in the synagogue's assembly hall or in a room adjoining it.

In the Jerusalem Talmud the question is raised: "In a town in which all the residents are priests, when they spread their hands [in the synagogue] and give the priestly blessing, who responds 'Amen'?" (The priests themselves are not permitted to give the response to their own blessing.) The answer is: "The women and children." Although not the point of the discussion, this rabbinic ruling indicates that women were in attendance at the synagogue. [39]

Author Shmuel Safrai explains that there was no separation

---

[39] The Place of Women in First-century Synagogues: They were much more active in religious life than they are today - CBE International

of men and women in the Temple in the 1st Century. Women were equals to men. Safrai explains that women were allowed in every area of the Temple precincts in which men were allowed. Although it is often thought that the women were to remain in the Women's Court, this area was not reserved for women. Both men and women went here. Public assemblies took place in the Women's Court. And remember, Yeshua treated the women with utmost respect. There was no separation of the sexes in synagogues, and women could be counted as part of the required congregational minimum of ten adults. Women were in leadership and named disciples, apostles, and prophets in the Book of Acts, but in Rabbinical Judaism, a woman cannot judge disputes in Torah law. How does one make light of Deborah, the Judge and prophetess who sat under her palm tree, and the people came to her for advice, wisdom, and knowledge just as they did Moses? Is wisdom limited to the male population? Certain rabbis even claim that there must have been men sitting under the palm tree with her:

> Rabeinu Asher writes that Devorah {Deborah} could not have been judging disputes herself, since women are not permitted to judge. Rather, she must have been instructing male judges how they should judge. [40]

Women throughout the ages have been suppressed and considered inferior to men. This type of perception needs

---

[40] Why Are There No Female Judges in Torah? - Chabad.org

correction. In the church, women are often placed in charge of changing diapers or teaching the younger children. Why haven't men realized that although they may think women today should not teach or are unqualified, children are not prejudiced and they are like sponges, soaking up the knowledge these women provide.

I distinctly remember the day I went to my pastor years ago about a matter on my heart. I looked him in the eye and said, "I feel the Holy One has called me to teach the Gospel." My pastor looked at me sorrowfully and shook his head, "Tekoa, God will never bless it." I felt like someone had stabbed me in the heart. "Why, not," I pleaded. He proceeded to show me scripture after scripture to prove his point. The primary scripture used was: "But I do not allow a woman to teach or exercise authority over a man, but to remain quiet" (I Timothy 2:12, TLV). And yet, Paul was always for women being used in ministry. Paul often spoke highly of the women in positions of authority, and he listed eight women in Romans Chapter sixteen that were of honor and in leadership:

> With this letter, I'm introducing Phoebe to you. She is our sister in the Christian faith and a deacon of the church in the city of Cenchrea.
>
> –Romans 16:1, GWT
>
> Greet Mary, who has worked hard for you.
>
> –Romans 16:6, NASB

Greet Andronicus and Junia, my kinsfolk and my fellow prisoners, who are outstanding in the view of the apostles, who also were in Christ before me.

–Romans 16:7, NASB

Greet Tryphaena and Tryphosa, workers in the Lord.

–Romans 16:12, NASB

Greet Prisca and Aquila, my fellow workers in Christ Jesus, who for my life risked their own necks, to whom not only do I give thanks, but also all the churches of the Gentiles; also greet the church that is in their house.

–Romans 16:3-5, NASB

Priscilla (Prisca) and her husband illustrate and teach the gospel together to a man in the synagogue. Paul, the same apostle who said, "I suffer not a woman to teach," writes about Priscilla, who taught very well:

Now a Jew named Apollos, an Alexandrian by birth, an eloquent man, came to Ephesus; and he was proficient in the Scriptures. This man had been instructed in the way of the Lord; and being fervent in spirit, he was accurately speaking and teaching things about Jesus, being acquainted only with the baptism of John; and he began speaking boldly in the synagogue. But when Priscilla and

Aquila heard him, they took him aside and explained the way of God more accurately to him.

–Acts 18:24-26, NASB

Paul informs us in Acts 18 that Priscilla and her husband were teaching and showing a man, "Apollos," a better understanding of the Messiah. Also, worth noting is the fact that despite being named after a pagan Greek god, Apollos never changed his name, and nobody had a meltdown over it. Apollos was humble enough to receive higher knowledge from a woman.

Was the Apostle Paul speaking out of both sides of his mouth? In I Timothy 2:12, Paul says, "I suffer not a woman to teach." Why is that? Paul was talking about one woman and not women in general. He was correcting a woman who was usurping and out of order in the congregation of Ephesus. And Paul gives hints to some of the issues in Chapter one:

> Just as I urged you upon my departure for Macedonia, to remain on at Ephesus so that you would instruct certain people not to teach strange doctrines nor to pay attention to myths and endless genealogies which give rise to useless speculation rather than advance the plan of God, which is by faith, so I urge you now.

–I Timothy 1:3-4, NASB

Reading I and II Timothy in their entirety teaches more about the people and culture of that time. The letters written by

Paul throughout much of the New Testament reveal several problems concerning female goddesses. Ephesus, where Timothy had started his assembly, was a well-known place of goddess worship. The temples erected in Ephesus (Western Turkey) were for the goddess of Artemis and Diana. Artemis's temple was one of the *Seven Wonders of the World*. The goddess was adorned on merchandise such as necklaces and bracelets as an idol and a statue to place in one's home. Alexander, the blacksmith, made his money from making these idols. Paul was putting a damper on Alexander the coppersmith's business by preaching the gospel and having the people put away their idols and burn their magic books of enchantment and witchcraft. Paul said, "Alexander the coppersmith did me much evil: the Father reward him according to his works" (II Timothy 4:14, KJV).

The people of Ephesus were Romans and Greeks, and they had been worshipping the goddess Artemis for over a thousand years. The goddess Diana (Asherah/Ashtoreth) that Jezebel worshipped was often referred to as the Queen of Heaven. In Jeremiah 7 the prophet Jeremiah mentions her:

> The children gather wood, the fathers kindle the fire, and the women knead dough to make sacrificial cakes for the queen of heaven [they still make those for Ashurah in Islam]; and they pour out drink offerings to other gods in order to provoke Me to anger.
>
> –Jeremiah 7:18, NASB

Those in Ephesus thought Diana created the world of her own being, having in herself the seeds of all creation yet to come. The people believed everyone came from her womb, and she was created first, according to them. Paul had to get strict with the Church of Ephesus because they were taking their goddess cult and mingling it with the truth of Adonai's Word.

The women were dressing like the goddess. Paul corrected them and told them they did not need braided hair and gold and extravagant attire. The women were not wearing braids like the television show *Little House on the Prairie*. They were dressed like their idol. It was no different than a young girl today dressing like one of her favorite pop stars:

> Likewise, women are to adorn themselves in appropriate clothing with modesty and sound judgment—not in seductive hairstyles and gold or pearls or costly clothing, but what is suitable for women claiming godliness, through good deeds.
>
> –I Timothy 2:9-10, TLV

Going back to the main verse I Timothy 2:12 as a proof text, the idea that women are unfit to teach the Gospel does not work. The verse cannot stand alone when we have women in ministry throughout the Gospels and the Book of Acts. Women are being used in house assemblies, as disciples, apostles, and prophets throughout the Newer Testament. How can we unravel I Timothy and the message of women staying silent in the assemblies? Dr. Skip Moen wrote an intriguing Book, *Guardian Angel,* which enlightens the role of women in the 1st Century and how that role has been misconstrued over time and looked at through a Greek lens. Moen rationalizes how Paul deliberately switches from the plural "women" when he talks about godly behavior for the whole congregation to the singular "woman" when he encourages Timothy in the Book of 1st Timothy 2:12. Dr. Moen explains how Paul has one specific woman in mind. This woman has caused disturbances and distress among the Body of Messiah, but the apostle does not reveal her name. Dr. Moen gives further information on Greek thought in his article *Unnamed, Hebrew Word Study*:

> For more than a thousand years, the Church employed a Greek philosophical paradigm when it interpreted this verse. That Greek model comes directly from Plato and Aristotle who taught that women were *defective* men. It isn't too much of an exaggeration to say Greek philosophers despised women, considering them intellectually inferior, emotionally immature and generally incapable of the actions and attitudes of men. The early church fathers were immersed in Greek philosophy, so it is not surprising to find their exegesis reflects Plato and the Academy. As a result of this paradigm, the Church and the culture engaged in withholding education, development, and leadership

from women. Predictably, the result merely confirmed what the paradigm taught: women were inferior. [41]

This paradigm often led to much homosexuality as the Romans believed women were so inferior to men that love could only be found in another man, since love requires an equal.

As a result of false traditions of men and passages taken out of context, my pastor believed, and told me, that women under no circumstances could be teachers. But it was not only from him; I found opposition everywhere. I watched as men with little to no biblical knowledge were placed in leadership roles. After approaching another pastor, I was informed that a single woman was dangerous in ministry. He said, "under no circumstances should a woman be placed in such an office, not even in youth ministry." The response to me was "A woman needs a covering to preach, and a husband is her covering." I was then directed to read a passage from Paul's letter written to an assembly in Corinth:

> And I wish you to know that the head of every man is the Messiah, and the head of the woman is the man, and the head of Messiah is Elohim. Every man praying or prophesying, having his head covered, brings shame to his head. And every woman praying or prophesying with her

---

[41] <u>The Unnamed | Hebrew Word Study | Skip Moen</u>

head uncovered brings shame to her head, for that is one and the same as if her head were shaved.

–I Corinthians 11:3-5, ISR

The passage from I Corinthians 11 is ambiguous. The term "head covering" has been made into a plethora of doctrines. When studying I Corinthians 11 with 1st Century biblical knowledge, we realize men did not have long hair. Men had facial hair, but they did not have the flowing long hair Jesus is depicted with in many paintings. When considering I Corinthians 11 and headscarves, we cannot leave out that Paul may have been confirming the teachings found in the Torah that warn against a man dressing like a woman, or a woman dressing like a man, and further the hair styles:

A woman shall not wear a man's garment, nor shall a man put on a woman's cloak, for whoever does these things is an abomination to the LORD your God.

–Deuteronomy 22:5, ESV

Compare the passage in Deuteronomy with Paul's words to those in Corinth:

Every man who prays or prophesies with his head covered dishonors his head. And every woman who prays or prophesies with her head uncovered dishonors her head, for it is just as if her head were shaved.

–I Corinthians 11:4-5, BSB

Continuing in I Corinthians 11:

> Judge for yourselves: is it proper for a woman to pray to
> Elohim with her head uncovered? Does not nature itself
> teach you that if a man indeed has long hair, it is a
> disrespect to him? And if a woman has long hair, it is an
> esteem to her, because the long hair has been given to her
> over against a veil. If, however, anyone seems to be
> contentious, we do not have such a habit, nor do the
> assemblies of Elohim.
>
> −I Corinthians 11:13-16, ISR

Paul states that long hair on a man during that time is a
"disrespect" to him. A Jewish Nazarite vow required a male to
grow his hair. In Acts18.18, Paul himself took this vow which
confirms his hair was short and that men's hair was indeed kept
trimmed, unless they were called Samson. Even so, the customs
and culture in Corinth in the 1ˢᵗ Century may have differed from
the Jewish traditions. Since Paul is answering a letter from the
leaders in Corinth, and we do not have the letter he received at
our disposal, we can only surmise by the clues we read in the
epistle. We know that sexual immorality was discussed as well as
idolatry and drunkenness in chapter 5 of 1ˢᵗ Corinthians. And
further reading in I Corinthians, discloses the goddess worship
and the belief that the woman was created before the man. Paul
must debunk all the pagan teachings and rituals. He must give
instructions on headship.

Grace in Torah Author and teacher, Kisha Gallagher expounds on this in her series, The Biblical Role of Women:

> If there was no hierarchy in the beginning, then men are only the "head" in the sense of order in the creation, not rank. While this rubs against a lot of traditional theology, I urge you to explore this idea more fully before rejecting it off hand.
>
> If man was meant to rule over or master women from the beginning, why does Paul in Ephesians chapter 5 instruct the women to *submit* to their husbands? Carefully consider this. We mustn't allow current doctrine or tradition to define this for us; rather, we must take the whole of Scripture into consideration and let it interpret itself. Though the difference may be "subtle", it has far reaching implications. The woman must choose to give her husband authority just as we must choose to give Messiah (Christ) authority over our lives. A man doesn't naturally possess the position of head by the simple fact that he is *male*.
>
> So why does the wife submit? This action only works properly if the man also does what Paul requires: *love his wife*. If a man really loves a woman, he's willing to do anything for her—- *even die* (Ephesians 5:25). This is a selfless type of love. If a woman is loved in this way, she naturally gives the man authority. She trusts that he will

always have her best interests at heart. The authority she gives protects her; it doesn't control or silence her. [42]

The Messiah is the head of the assembly, which means He protects, provides, and nourishes His Body just as a husband protects, supplies, and nourishes his wife and vice versa. The two become one flesh.

It was not only a head covering I was told I needed; it felt like an all-out assault against every woman I had ever loved in the Bible. From Anna, the prophetess who prophesied over the Messiah, to Deborah, the brave judge, who could forget the woman at the well who led her whole town to the Lord. After telling two pastors about the most resounding cry of my heart and being met with opposition, I went to the Holy One in prayer, and I fell on my face and asked Him why He had given me the vision and the desire if these men were right. The Father led me to the Book of Job. After Job's troubles, Adonai restores everything that Job lost. Job had seven sons and three daughters, but the Bible does not mention his sons' names, only his daughters. The Hebrew culture takes names very seriously. Adonai changed Abram's name, and the very breath of the Father was injected into his name. Abram became Abraham as Adonai inserted the fifth letter of the Hebrew alphabet, the *hey*, into his name. The letter *hey* represents God's creative power and His very Breath. Abraham's character changed, so he needed a new

---

[42] The Biblical Role of Women Part VII | GRACE in TORAH

name to convey his character. Jacob left his name, which meant trickster, and was given the name Israel after wrestling with an angel. Jacob then had a name that meant "one who prevails with Adonai." Inspecting Job's daughters' names conveys more about these women by applying the same tools:

> And he called the name of the first Jemima; and the name of the second, Kezia; and the name of the third, Keren-happuch.
>
> –Job 42:14, KJV

Jemima, according to *BDB Theological Dictionary*, means Dove. Still, *Abarim Publications* explains that most ancient translations of the Bible derive the name Jemimah from the noun יום (yom), meaning a day. The derived adverb יומם (yomam) means by day, or during daylight. That would give the name Jemimah the pleasing meaning of "Lady Daylight." The second name Kezia means cassia, a sweet-scented spice. Keren-happuch means to shine, the horn of beauty, or alloys of medicine. When the Father led me to the daughters of Job and their name meanings, the following verse popped off the page:

> And in all the land were no women found so fair as the daughters of Job: and their father gave them inheritance among their brethren.
>
> –Job 42:15, KJV

Women everywhere have an inheritance with their brothers!

The Father has always sought help from his daughters. He called Miriam, Moses' sister, to help lead the children of Israel through the wilderness. Miriam was a mighty prophetess. During the time of Jeremiah, we see rulers seeking out a female prophetess named Huldah. She warned them of the destruction that was coming because of idolatry. The men could have sought out Jeremiah instead:

> So Hilkiah the kohen, Ahikam, Achbor, Shaphan, and Asaiah went to Huldah the prophetess, the wife of Shallum son of Tikvah, son of Harhas, keeper of the wardrobe—she was living in the Second Quarter of Jerusalem—and spoke with her.
>
> —II Kings 22:14, TLV

The Holy One appointed Esther to save His people, and she called for a three-day fast, not even water. Esther risked her life for Adonai's people. Let us not forget Moses' wife, Zipporah, who spared Moses from death when God wished to kill him because he had not circumcised their sons. Deborah was a prophetess and a judge who gave battle strategies for Israel because the men would not. Deborah knew the Torah, and the men and women came to her as the people had come to Moses for counsel because Deborah was equal to him:

> Deborah the wife of Lappidoth was a prophet and a leader of Israel during those days. She would sit under Deborah's

Palm Tree between Ramah and Bethel in the hill country of Ephraim, where Israelites would come and ask her to settle their legal cases.

–Judges 4:4-5, CEV

And let us not forget Yael, who put a tent peg through a wicked king's head.

But as he lay sleeping from exhaustion, Heber's wife Jael took a tent peg, grabbed a hammer, and went silently to Sisera. She drove the peg through his temple and into the ground, and he died.

–Judges 4:21, BSB

Women continue to shine throughout the whole Bible. The first woman evangelist in the Gospel of John was the woman at the well. She took the living water of Yeshua Messiah and ran to tell everyone in her town, and many believed. "And many of the Samaritans of that city believed on Him for the saying of the woman, which testified, He told me all that ever I did" (John 4:39, KJV).

In Luke 8, the Messiah had several women right there with him, and the text implies that they ministered to Him:

Soon afterward, *Yeshua* began traveling throughout towns and villages, preaching and proclaiming the Good News of the Kingdom of God. The twelve were also with Him. And certain women who had been healed of evil spirits and infirmities—Miriam, the one called Magdalene, out of whom seven demons had gone; Joanna, the wife of Kuza, Herod's finance minister; Susanna; and many others—were supporting the twelve and Yeshua out of their own resources.

–Luke 8:1-3, TLV

Additionally, not only are women named disciples in scripture, we read of a female apostle named Junia in the Book of Acts and the Book of Romans:

Now there was at Joppa a certain disciple named Tabitha, which by interpretation is called Dorcas: this woman was full of good works and alms deeds which she did.

–Acts 9:36, KJV

Greet Andronicus and Junia, my fellow Jews who have been in prison with me. They are outstanding among the apostles, and they were in Christ before I was.

–Romans 16:7, NIV

Today, the Holy One has poured out His spirit on all flesh. I hope that Adonai's handmaidens everywhere are encouraged to step out in faith and proceed to heed His calling. Avoid the naysayers, for they will always be present. The Father is using many of His called-out ones in this hour, just as He used Deborah, Esther, Rahab, and Ruth. Men, be careful not to overlook the voices of women in your congregations. Our Father has given them gifts and roles in the Body of Messiah, and He will continue to make room for them.

Wolves Unseen: Book Three

Chapter 7

THE HARLOT CHURCH

Today's news is full of violence, wars, pandemics, sexual perversion; and a world that lacks wisdom, knowledge, and understanding. When watching such matters, it can be easy to point at the world with all its darkness and think, "I am glad I am not like those people!" But it's not just the world that has problems. The "church" is full of many perversions that are covert and hidden, and many of the leaders are wolves in sheep's clothing. Often the people enticed by them are young and naive, not realizing they are part of a harlot system.

In the Book of Proverbs, the characteristics of a harlot are unveiled. When reading, envision the religious church system. The Book of Proverbs is not about a prostitute on the corner, but the author used a harlot as a symbol. The harlot is seductive. Remember, the adversary often comes as an angel of light (2 Corinthians 11:14). The harlot comes out in the darkest hours of the night, and the world keeps growing darker and darker. In those days harlotry was not just concerning a profession for wayward women; it was someone not honoring vows, especially marriage (Covenant) vows. The harlot in the Book of Revelation and Proverbs concerns a woman in covenant with Adonai, who was acting in a manner of an adulterous bride:

> For at the window of my house I looked out through my lattice. I saw among the naïve, I noticed among the youth, a young man lacking understanding, crossing the street near her corner, walking in the direction of her house, in the twilight of the evening, in the darkest hours of the night. All of a sudden, a woman meets him, dressed as a prostitute and with a cunning heart. She is loud and defiant. Her feet never stay at home— now in the streets, now in the squares, at every corner she lurks.
>
> –Proverbs 7:6-8, TLV

Proverbs 7:6 begins the portion concerning the enticement of the harlot, but at the beginning of the chapter, Solomon tells the reader the key to not being seduced by this woman. He mimics the words of Yeshua, "If you love Me, you will keep My commandments" (John 14:15, BSB). These are the terms of the marriage covenant:

> My son, keep my words and treasure my mitzvot my (Commandments/Torah) within you. Keep my mitzvot and live, my teaching as the apple of your

eye. Bind them on your fingers, write them on the tablet of your heart.

–Proverbs 7:1-3, TLV

Sadly, the "church" has not done this. The harlot system has infiltrated the world and its leaders. The harlot system is likened to Pharaoh, who would not let God's people go. This system wants to enslave the people underneath them. Pharoah wants the people to be dependent on Egypt. Everything in spiritual Egypt is filled with falseness. The land and rulers of Egypt play on people's beastly appetites and desires for wealth, prestige, titles, sexual lust, pride, arrogance, self-seeking, being lovers of pleasure rather than lovers of God. Egypt injects fear. I'm not referring to the country, Egypt. No, Egypt, the nation, was once a place of refuge for the Holy One's people, but metaphorically, Egypt represents slavery, darkness, and false idols. This harlot system is filled with taskmasters, bondage, big pharmaceutical drug addiction, and idol worship. This beastly system does not just infect the world; it has crept into the church/synagogue and our institutions with over 40,000 denominations. It divides and conquers. This harlot system causes the people under its rulership to lose their identity and the true identity of the Messiah Yeshua. The Bride of Messiah was ingrafted into a living, breathing Israel. Although we are connected to the land of Israel, Israel is not simply a land mass. There is a spiritual Israel:

If the first fruit is holy, so is the whole batch of dough; and if the root is holy, so are the branches. But if some of the branches were broken off and you—being a wild olive—were grafted in among them and became a partaker of the root of the olive tree with its richness, do not boast against the branches. But if you do boast, it is not you who support the root but the root supports you.

–Romans 11: 16-18, TLV

Instead of our heritage, we have been taught a Greek Messiah who looks nothing like the Messiah, Yeshua, from the tribe of Judah. If the root supports us, we must tap into the olive oil and the tree. Christianity has removed itself far from the root system and, over time, invited the harlot in.

In Proverbs 7 the harlot grabs the naive young man and kisses him, and she has perfumed her bed. She has prepared her house with all the arousal of fine wine, bread, and Egyptian linens. Just like King Saul whose life ended sitting on the witch of Endor's bed and then sharing his last meal with her, the harlot captures the weak and naive:

So she grabs him and kisses him and with a brazen face says to him: "I had to sacrifice fellowship offerings; today I paid my vow. So I've come out to meet you, to seek your presence eagerly—and I found you! I have spread my couch with tapestry of dyed Egyptian linens. I have perfumed my bed with myrrh, aloes, and cinnamon. Come, let's drink our fill of love till morning! Let's delight ourselves with love. For my husband is not at home—he's gone on a long journey. He took a bag of money with him—he won't come home until full moon." With her persistent pleading she entices him, with smooth talk she seduces him. Suddenly he follows her like an ox going to the slaughter, like a stag bounding toward a trap, till an arrow pierces its liver. Like a bird darting into a snare, he never considered his own soul!

–Proverbs 7:13-22, TLV

Have we considered our souls? Proverbs 8 compares wisdom from above to the simple who have crossed the street and turned the corner into deep darkness. Proverbs 7 and 8 have many similarities, but the main one to emphasize is the similarity between the "church" and the brazen harlot.

The harlot grabs those who are unlearnt—those who do not know wisdom, knowledge, or understanding. The person is broken, "young" or immature and naive. Remember, the man was out at night, walking in the darkness. In verse 8, the man is near her house. In verse 9, we learn it is the twilight of the evening, the time of the evening sacrifice when the man would have been at the synagogue or temple or altar. This circumstance is a reminder of King David who should have been at war in the spring but instead walked on the roof top and spotted a woman bathing that was beautiful to behold. In Proverbs 7, the man is lurking by the home of the harlot in the darkest hours of the night, and he crosses the street. Crossing the street denotes going to the other side. Have you ever gotten too close to the fire? Or too close to pornography, gambling, drugs, idolatry, or committing adultery by walking closer and closer to the enticing harlot's house?

The Bride of Messiah is to walk in the light as He is in the light:

> And this is the message we have heard from Him and announce to you: God is light, and in Him there is no darkness at all. If we say we have fellowship with Him yet walk in the darkness, we lie and do not practice the truth. But if we walk in the light as He is in the light, we have fellowship with one another, and the blood of Jesus His Son cleanses us from all sin.
>
> –I John 1:5-7, BSB

In Proverbs 7:14 the harlot tells him that she has paid her fellowship/peace offering according to Leviticus 3:1, and that she has come to find him. The "strange" woman has sacrificed an offering. In her mind, she has paid her vows.

Continuing with Proverbs 7, repeating verses 18-22, the harlot says:

> Come, let's drink our fill of love till morning! Let's delight ourselves with love. For my husband is not at home—he's

gone on a long journey. He took a bag of money with him—he won't come home until full moon." With her persistent pleading she entices him, with smooth talk she seduces him.

Who is her husband? She tells the man that he is gone on a long journey. This sounds very similar to a parable Yeshua told:

> Keep on the lookout! Stay alert! For you do not know when the time is. It is like a man away on a journey. After leaving his house and putting his servants in charge and giving each his task, he also commanded the doorkeeper to watch. Therefore stay alert, for you do not know when the master of the house is coming, whether in the evening, at midnight, when the rooster crows, or in the early morning. So watch in case, coming suddenly, he finds you asleep. What I say to you I say to all: 'Stay alert!'"
>
> –Mark 13:33-37, TLV

In many parables Yeshua told, he is on a journey: "For the kingdom of heaven is like a man traveling to a far country, who called his own servants and delivered his goods to them" (Matthew 25:14 KJV).

In Proverbs 7:20, the promiscuous woman tells the man that her husband took a bag of money with him and will not be back until the full moon. There is only one feast that falls on the full moon: Passover. Scholars are unsure if this translation is correct since it was so dark outside. Is Proverbs 7, hinting at a new moon and the fall feasts, such as Yom Teruah, the Feast of Trumpets, when we watch for the return of the Messiah. Author of *Grace in Torah* and *The Biblical New Moon*, Kisha Gallagher explains why the Feast of Trumpets is called a hidden day that no man knows, referring to the Day of the Lord in her blog series *Moonbeams and Moedim:*

> Although Chanukah extends into a new moon phase, there is only one feast day that begins at the New Moon: *Yom Teruah* or Rosh Hashanah (Trumpets). It may now be very obvious why trumpets are blown at this date. Since weather can affect the sighting of a new moon sliver, this day has been dubbed, *Yom HaKeseh,* the Hidden Day at which no man knows the hour or the day of its occurrence. *Yom Teruah* heralds the seventh month, the coming Day of Atonement, and the Feast of Ingathering.
>
> This day calls the ones sleeping in darkness to hear the great alarm of the shofar. Wake from slumber and know the season and phase you are entering. The Father desires that none perish, but many will choose otherwise. There are exactly ten days between Rosh Hashanah and Yom Kippur. These days are called the Days of Awe and throughout this time, the moon grows fuller and fuller. In

other words, the new moon ɔrings promises of more light, more awareness. [43]

Both the harlot and the wise woman are described as searching in the streets (Proverbs 7:12, 8:2,3). The wise woman and the harlot, both, are inviting men into their homes. The harlot has a table, and the Lord has a table. Remember Jezebel's table had false prophets dining at her table:

1. **The harlot has an invitation:** "Come, let us take our fill of love till morning. Let us delight in loving caresses!" (Proverbs 7:19).

2. **The voice of wisdom has an invitation:** The wise build their house by keeping the commandments and staying awake and watching for the return of their husband, Yeshua. "Blessed is the man who listens to me, watching daily at my doors, waiting at the posts of my doorway" (Proverbs 8:34).

3. **The harlot is roaming the streets**: "Then a woman came out to meet him, with the attire of a harlot and cunning of heart. She is loud and defiant; her feet do not remain at home. Now in the street, now in the squares, she lurks at every corner" (Proverbs 7:10-12).

4. **Wisdom is crying out in the streets:** "Does not wisdom call out, and understanding raise her voice?   On the heights overlooking the road, at the crossroads she

---

[43] Moonbeams and the Moedim Part II | GRACE in TORAH

takes her stand. Beside the gates to the city, at the entrances she cries out" (Proverbs 8:2-3).

5. **Wisdom's mouth**: The harlot has lips and wisdom has lips – "Listen, for I speak of noble things, and the opening of my lips will reveal right. For my mouth will speak the truth, and wickedness is detestable to my lips. All the words of my mouth are righteous; none are crooked or perverse. They are all plain to the discerning, and upright to those who find knowledge. Receive my instruction instead of silver, and knowledge rather than pure gold. For wisdom is more precious than rubies, and nothing you desire compares with her" (Proverbs 8:7-11).

6. **The harlot's seductive mouth:** "She seizes him and kisses him; With her great persuasion she entices him; with her flattering lips she lures him. He follows her on impulse" (Proverbs 7:13, 21-22).

All of us flirt with other lovers—walk too close to the flames. We all are guilty. Have Adonai's people forsaken their identities and been swept up and enticed by men who have preached another gospel. Paul warns of this very thing:

For if someone comes and proclaims another Yeshua whom we did not proclaim, or if you receive a different spirit that you did not receive, or a different "good news" that you did not accept, you put up with that well enough! For I consider myself in no way inferior to the "super special" emissaries. Even if I am unskilled in speech, yet I am not so in knowledge. No, in every way we have made this clear to you in all things.

–II Corinthians. 11:4-6, TLV

Listen to the voice of the harlot in the following dialogue between two famous television evangelists/pastors who distort the truth and bring itching ear words—words that tickle the ear. The message of salvation in many circles has been changed into a prosperity message of abundance full of false doctrines of men and the voice of the harlot. Here is a conversation I typed verbatim from a televised segment:

> **Speaker #1:** People told me, 'Well, they say, Jesus was poor.' When was He poor? I would like to know when He was poor. Well, He was born in a stable. Why? Why was He born in a stable? Because that short, deaf lady lost their reservation. He couldn't get into the inn. Think about that for a minute. And He had twelve full-time people on His staff. Some were married, and He took care of them. He had seventy part-timers. You don't gamble for rags.
>
> **Speaker #2:** Yeah.
>
> **Speaker #1:** You don't gamble for rags. You gamble for some clothes that cost. Don't you? He wanted a donkey that had never been ridden. As I said earlier, 'You might want a car that has never been driven.'

Speaker #2: He had a full-time treasurer on staff.

Speaker #1: That's right! And he stole for three years, and the other guys didn't know about it.

Speaker #2: And wise men came to see Him.

Speaker #1: That's right! I mean, He wasn't three minutes on the ground, and the three wise guys are looking for Him with what? Gold, Frankincense, and Myrrh. Let me tell you something, this concept that Jesus was in poverty is totally wrong!

Sadly, once more, these are not biblical truths. These words are itching ear words that tickle desires in those who are seeking after the things of this world, but this type of preaching is nothing more than the voice of the harlot.

Point One: Yeshua was not born in a stable. He was born in a cave or tower, as the prophet Micah and others prophesied. Clay Mize author of *The Power of Humility*, explains more in his blogpost *Lamb of God – The manger in Migdal Eder:*

> Although the Newer Testament does not tell us where in Bethlehem Yeshua was born, the Older Testament (Tanakh) does. Micah 4:8 states, "And thou, O tower of the flock, the strong hold of the daughter of Zion, unto thee shall it come, even the first dominion; the kingdom shall come to the daughter of Jerusalem." The Messiah

would be born at the "tower of the flock." (Hebrew: Migdal Edar). [44]

Continuing with the location, we learn that Rachel was buried here after giving birth to Benjamin, Son of my Right Hand. Yeshua sits at the right hand of God:

> So Rachel died and was buried on the way to Ephrath (that is, Bethlehem). Jacob set up a pillar over her grave; that is the pillar of Rachel's grave to this day. Then Israel journeyed on and pitched his tent beyond the tower of Eder.
>
> –Genesis 35:19-21, NASB

After burying Rachel, Jacob moved his flocks beyond the tower of Eder. This would pinpoint the location near what is known today as Bethlehem. This watchtower from ancient times was where ewes were safely brought to give birth to lambs. In this sheltered building/cave, the priests would bring in the ewes about to give birth. These new babies had a critical call. These were special lambs from a unique flock designated for sacrifice at the Temple in Jerusalem.

Rabbi Mike L. Short, author and teacher at *B'Seder* (Everything's fine), illustrates more concerning these special lambs in his teaching *Migdal Eder*:

---

[44] http://powerofhumility.org/migdal-eder/

According to Edersheim in *The Life And Times Of Jesus The Messiah,* in Book 2, Chapter 6, states, "This Migdal Edar was not the watchtower for the ordinary flocks that pastured on the barren sheep ground beyond Bethlehem, but it lay close to the town, on the road to Jerusalem. A passage from the Mishnah (Shekelim 7:4) leads to the conclusion that the flocks which pastured there were destined for Temple sacrifices. [45]

Gathering this information, we learn that Yeshua was brought into the tower, the exact place for birthing baby ewes. These lambs would be carefully cared for because one day they would be the Passover lambs, just as Yeshua was our Passover Lamb. It is this divine place that Joseph took his wife Mary (Miriam), and it is no mistake that there was no room in the inn.

The shepherds of these lambs were the elite shepherds from the priestly tribe of Levi, whose job was to care for them so they would remain without blemish or spot. Although there is no historical proof, it has been said that from the birth of a lamb, they were spoiled, wrapped in fine linen to remain without blemish and imperfection, and fed a special diet.

Point Two: The Bible never states that there were three wise men (Magi). Their ancestors were trained by the prophet Daniel in his role as the chief Magi. We do not know the number of men, but we do read of three gifts that may have, in fact, been

---

[45] Migdal Eder QRcode generator (mayimhayim.org)

one gift. (Matthew 2:1). One fascinating article by Chaim Ben Torah, *The Gift of the Magi*, explains that possibly the Magi only brought one gift. The Aramaic word used for gift is *qorbana*. Chaim explains that this word is misleading. The word *qorbana* comes from the word corban, which Yeshua used in Matthew 15:6, where he rebukes the Pharisees for calling their offering a corban. Chaim Ben Torah explains this conundrum and the singular gift of the Magi:

> A corban is literally an offering or sacrifice to God. It could be an animal sacrifice, or an incense offering, which was most likely the case here. Frankincense or myrrh were used only in the Holy of Holies and was mixed in a golden vessel and burned on a golden plate. You see, the gold, frankincense, and myrrh were not the gifts given by the wise men. They burned up the frankincense and myrrh and most likely took the golden cups and plates home with them to continue to burn their oils and worship God. Mary and Joseph didn't take the oils and the gold and sell them for passage to Egypt as that was not the gift that the Magi gave to Jesus. The Gift of the Magi was a hazardous journey untaken for only one purpose found in Matthew 2:2, "We are come to worship Him." [46]

---

[46] http://www.chaimbentorah.com/2014/12/word-study-gift-magi/

Yeshua was no longer a newborn at this point. He was a child closer to two years of age, and he lived in a house:

> After listening to the king, they went their way. And behold, the star they had seen in the east went on before them, until it came to rest over the place where the Child was. When they saw the star, they rejoiced exceedingly with great gladness. And when they came into the house, they saw the Child with His mother Miriam; and they fell down and worshiped Him.
>
> –Matthew 2:9-11, TLV

The "church" must stop supporting and sitting under the harlot. The apostles and prophets, those who came before us, those martyred for the sake of the Gospel, did not suffer so that we can live life in wealth and pleasure. The chapter headings below from the New Testament are a testimony in themselves:

1. The Apostles Imprisoned

2. The Arrest of Stephen

3. The Stoning of Stephen

4. Paul and Silas Imprisoned

5. The Plot to Kill Paul

There are no references to them living comfortably and amassing wealth:

But they that will be rich, fall into temptation and a snare, and into many foolish and hurtful lusts, which drown men in destruction and perdition.

−I Timothy 6:9, KJV

The Book of Hebrews has a sobering chapter that reads like The Book of Martyrs:

Women received their dead raised to life again: and others were tortured, not accepting deliverance; that they might obtain a better resurrection: and others had trial of cruel mocking, and scourging, yea, moreover of bonds and imprisonment: They were stoned, they were sawn asunder, were tempted, were slain with the sword: they wandered about in sheepskins and goatskins; being destitute, afflicted, tormented; of whom the world was not worthy.

−Hebrews 11:35-38, KJV

Yeshua had more to say about wealth and riches in the book of Revelation, and it is a far cry from what the wolves are feeding the flock today:

Because you say, "I am rich, and have become wealthy, and have need of nothing," and you do not know that you are wretched and miserable and poor and blind and naked.

−Revelation 3:17, NASB

145

Yeshua then tells the church of Smyrna this: "I know your tribulation and your poverty (but you are rich)!" Revelation 2:9, NASB). The opposite seems to be true. If you want to live, you must die. If you wish to receive, you must give. So, these rich people were impoverished, and the poor were wealthy.

Yeshua also talked about business and wealth and good stewardship too. And Solomon warns against being either too rich and becoming complacent or being too poor and living in shame. The Ebionites and Desert Fathers and Franciscans went to the other extreme, with poverty vows. Many became burdens on society which is also not loving their neighbor. Every kingdom needs finances to get the job done.

Use caution when listening to certain ministers because they may have the smooth enticing tongue of the harlot, but her roads lead to death. The harlot is loud, seductive, and has no room for introspection or repentance or studying like the Bereans. Proverbs 8 gives the ingredient for the beginning of wisdom: "The fear of *Adonai* is the beginning of wisdom and knowledge of the Holy One is understanding" (Proverbs 8:10, TLV). The word for "fear" in this context means being in awe of a holy God and treating Him with reverence. If we stay hidden under His Wings, we will be far from the harlot's seductive lips and loud voice in our ears.

Chapter 8

PERGAMUM, ANTIPAS, AND BALAAM

Pergamum is an archaeological site in present-day Turkey that developed under the Attalid dynasty following the death of Alexander the Great. Pergamum grew rich and powerful as an ancient Greek city. In Revelation 2, Yeshua tells the church of Pergamum that they dwell where Satan's throne is. This mysterious passage also mentions a martyr named Antipas. Dr. Tim Gibson, pastor and evangelist, describes the severity of idolatry present at Pergamum in his article *Pergamum - The church married to the world*. The Pergamum Museum is now in Berlin and has the Ishtar Gate:

> In all of Asia Minor (Turkey) this city was the most fanatical about Caesar worship. Caesar worship began under Augustus and the first temple built honoring this cult was in Pergamum in 27 BC. Two other temples were built honoring Trajan and Septimus Severus. Here

Christians were in danger of severe persecution year-round as a result of their refusal to participate in Caesar worship. As the primary religious center of Asia Minor, Pergamum also worshiped the usual pantheon of Greek gods and had temples dedicated to Athena, Asklepios, Dionysus and Zeus. In fact, Zeus is said to have been born there. The great altar stood on a foundation 125 ft by 115 ft, over 50 ft high, set in a colonnaded enclosure. [47]

Caesar worship is similar to what we see today in America. President Obama was called the messiah, a savior for the people. President Trump was placed in a position of a god that could save us and make our nation great again. The problem with these ideologies is no man of flesh can save us. In Revelation 2, we learn of a man named Antipas. Some historians believe Antipas was sentenced to death on the Altar of Zeus inside a brazen bull. This contraption was one of the evilest inventions of all time.

According to Diodorus Siculus, in 560 BC, Perilaus, a metalsmith from Athens, designed the brazen bull. Perilaus made the contraption for the Phalaris, the despot of the Sicilian city of Acragas. Phalaris was known for his excessive cruelty, so with this in mind, Perilaus designed something incredibly unpleasant for him to execute his enemies in. Ironically, legend holds that Perilaus ended up dying in the cruel contraption he built:

---

[47] Print (aplaceforyou.org)

As the name suggests, the brazen bull was a hollow metal vessel in the shape of a bull. The condemned were forced inside through a trapdoor in the bull's belly and then enclosed within. Once the victim was secured, a fire was lit beneath the bull, heating the metal—and cooking the unfortunate victim. Pipes fitted to the bull's mouth converted the sounds of the victim's agonized screams into: "the tenderest, most melodious, most pathetic of bellowing's" as Perilaus described them when he was pitching the bull to Phalaris. [48]

And so Antipas was killed where Satan dwells. This unusual description is mentioned in several other places, and Pergamum is said to be where Satan's throne is:

And to the angel of the church in Pergamum write: "The words of him who has the sharp two-edged sword." I know where you dwell, where Satan's throne is. Yet you hold fast my name, and you did not deny my faith even in the days of Antipas my faithful witness, who was killed among you, where Satan dwells. But I have a few things against you: you have some there who hold the teaching of Balaam, who taught Balak to put a stumbling block before the sons

---

[48] https://historycollection.com/12-torturous-methods-execution-history/7/

of Israel, so that they might eat food sacrificed to idols and practice sexual immorality.

–Revelation 2:12-14, ESV

Revelation 2 states that the assembly or church in Smyrna and Philadelphia were from the synagogue of Satan, and the community in Thyatira went after the deep things of Satan. The school of Hillel and the harsher school of Shammai were two schools that had drastically different rules concerning the engrafting of Gentiles into Judaism. The Sanhedrin, the council of the Jews, was controlled by a group of Pharisees known as the House of Shammai. The House of Shammai was anti-Gentile and enacted eighteen mandates that the opposing school, the House of Hillel, found so shameful they compared them to the golden calf at Sinai. (See Luke 13:16-24 concerning the woman that was bent over in bondage for 18 years). It was common in the time of Yeshua to refer to the Pharisees of Beit Shammai as the firstborn of Satan or the Synagogue of Satan. The reason was due to their hatred of non-Jews. For more on this topic, see Book One, *Satan Unmasked*, from this series, *Unmasking the Unseen*. However, the topic concerning Antipas dwelling where Satan's throne is differs from the school of Shammai. Also, much of Revelation is cryptic. Much of the language and setting in the Book of Revelation are a mystery. For example, the reader must unravel who the woman is sitting on a scarlet beast covered with names of blasphemy, having seven heads and ten horns in chapter 17.

Greg Beale, professor of New Testament and biblical theology at Westminster Theological Seminary, gives a more reasonable explanation behind the "throne of Satan" in his commentary, *The Book of Revelation (New International Greek Testament Commentary, pg. 246)*:

> "The throne of Satan" in Pergamum is a way of referring to that city as a center of Roman government and pagan religion in the Asia Minor region. It was the first city in Asia Minor to build a temple to a Roman ruler (Augustus) and the capital of the whole area for the cult of the emperor. The city proudly referred to itself as the "temple warden" (neokoros) of a temple dedicated to Caesar worship. Life in such a politico-religious center put all the more pressure on the church to pay public homage to Caesar as a deity, refusal of which meant high treason to the state.
>
> Furthermore, Pergamum was also a center of pagan cults of various deities. For example, the cult of Asclepius, the serpent god of healing, was prominent in Pergamum; the serpent symbol of Asclepius also became one of the emblems of the city and may have facilitated John's reference to "the throne of Satan" (cf. 12:9; 20:2). Zeus, Athene, Demeter, and Dionysus were also gods receiving significant cultic attention. [49]

---

[49] Revelation 2:13 / Satan's earthly headquarter? - Biblical Hermeneutics

According to Josephus, the Samaritans were the False Jews. They pretended to be Jews when it gained Roman favor and acted as Gentiles when it did not. They also had a counterfeit Temple and Holy City on Mount Gerizim.

The throne or seat of Satan represents totalitarian rule. The believers in Messiah who lived in Pergamum were under extreme cruelty and fearful situations. In an excerpt from the *Studies in Revelation* by Hamption Keathly III, a graduate of Dallas Theological Seminary and teacher at Moody Bible Institute, Keathly applies the throne of Satan to the pagan cults of many gods and, further, the pagan temple god whose idol was a serpent. Keathly goes further by explaining the Magian high priest who was referred to as "Chief Bridge Builder," meaning the one who spans the gap between mortals and Satan and his hosts:

> Pergamum was very wealthy, the center of emperor worship with many temples devoted to idolatry. This was the place "where Satan's throne is" (Rev. 2:13). The phrase has been applied to the complex of pagan cults, of Zeus, Athena, Dionysus, and Asclepius (Esculapius), established by the Attalid kings, that of Asclepius Soter (the "saviour," "healer") being of special importance. These cults are illustrative of the religious history of Pergamum, but "Satan's throne" could be an allusion to emperor worship. This was where the worship of the

divine emperor had been made the touchstone of civic loyalty under Domitian.

Here was the magnificent temple of Esculapius, a pagan god whose idol was in the form of a serpent. The inhabitants were known as the chief temple keepers of Asia. When the Babylonian cult of the Magians was driven out of Babylon, they found a haven in Pergamum.

And:

The title of the Magian high priest was "Chief Bridge Builder" meaning the one who spans the gap between mortals and Satan and his hosts. In Latin this title was written "Pontifex Maximus," the title now used by the Pope (same title as Constantine). This title goes all the way back to Babylon and the beginnings of the mother-child cult under Nimrod of Genesis 10 and his wife Sumerimus. Later, Julius Caesar was elected Pontifex Maximus and when he became Emperor, he became the supreme civil and religious ruler and head of Rome politically and religiously with all the power and functions of the Babylonian pontiff. [50]

Yeshua says that those in Pergamum hold fast to His Name even unto death. The Messiah knows about His faithful servant Antipas and what it was like for him to walk in faith unto death,

---

[50] Studies in Revelation | Bible.org

but Yeshua still has something against them, and instead of the Nicolaitans (*nico*/power, *laitans*/over people), it has to do with a prophet named Balaam.

Most people with any biblical background have heard of the story of Balaam, and if they do not remember him, they recognize his talking donkey. Balak was king of Moab, and he was intimidated by God's holy people, Israel. Balak sends messengers to summon Balaam, son of Beor a prophet, to come and speak curses over them:

> So he sent messengers to Balaam the son of Beor, at Pethor, which is near the River, in the land of the sons of his people, to call him, saying, "Behold, a people came out of Egypt; behold, they cover the surface of the land, and they are living opposite me." "Now, therefore, please come, curse this people for me since they are too mighty for me; perhaps I may be able to defeat them and drive them out of the land. For I know that he whom you bless is blessed, and he whom you curse is cursed.
>
> –Numbers 22:5-6, NASB

Abarim Publications defines the name of Balaam:

> The name Balaam means "not of the people or destroyer of the people," a foreigner. His father's name, Beor, means burning, torch or lamp. Balaam was a non-Israelite and a

diviner or fortune teller. He practiced witchcraft, and apparently, he was good at it. [51]

Numbers 7 gives a clue as to why Adonai hates this spirit. Like many false prophets today, Balaam charged a fee for his witchcraft: "The elders of Moab and Midian left with divination fees in their hand. When they came to Balaam, they told him Balak's words" (Numbers 22:7, TLV). The other perplexity concerning Balaam is that he heard from Adonai as a prophet. The conversation between Balaam and the Holy One is written in Numbers 22:

> Then God came to Balaam and said, "Who are these men with you?" Balaam said to God, "Balak the son of Zippor, king of Moab, has sent word to me, 'Behold, there is a people who came out of Egypt and they cover the surface of the land; now come, curse them for me; perhaps I may be able to fight against them and drive them out.'" God said to Balaam, "Do not go with them; you shall not curse the people, for they are blessed." So Balaam arose in the

---

[51] http://www.abarim-publications.com/Meaning/Balaam.html#.W-q1vE3QbRA

morning and said to Balak's leaders, "Go back to your land, for the LORD has refused to let me go with you."

–Numbers 22:9-13, NASB

The book of Jude lists multiple characteristics of Balaam, and much of it has to do with the love of money and pride:

> But these men revile the things which they do not understand; and the things which they know by instinct, like unreasoning animals, by these things they are destroyed. Woe to them! For they have gone the way of Cain, and for pay they have rushed headlong into the error of Balaam and perished in the rebellion of Korah. These are grumblers, finding fault, following after their own lusts; they speak arrogantly, flattering people for the sake of gaining an advantage.

–Jude 1:10, 11, 16, NASB

The book of II Peter warns the people, using Balaam as an example. Chapter 2 highlights false prophets and teachers, but interestingly, they are found among the church and the people:

> They count it a pleasure to revel in the daytime. They are stains and blemishes, reveling in their deceptions, as they carouse with you, having eyes full of adultery that never cease from sin, enticing unstable souls, having a heart trained in greed, accursed children; forsaking the right way, they have gone astray, having followed the way of

Balaam, the son of Beor, who loved the wages of unrighteousness; but he received a rebuke for his own transgression, for a mute donkey, speaking with a voice of a man, restrained the madness of the prophet.

–II Peter 2:13-16, NASB

These men are false prophets who love the spotlight and money. The word "antichrist" is layered. It can also mean a replacement, or "instead of" Christ." Christ or Messiah means "the anointed one." An antichrist is a counterfeit.

Brad Scott, author, and teacher of *Wildbranch Ministries* explains:

> In John's first epistle, we are told that there is an antichrist to come and is even now in the world as we speak. This word in Greek is *antichristos* (ἀντίχριστος). The word *anti* is a word that has several meanings but has come to be understood in our culture as something that opposes or is the opposite. However, that is not the biblical use of this word as it pertains to this entity that supposedly opposes the Messiah. The word also means *instead of* or *because of,* as well. The word comes from the Hebrew word *tachat* (תחת). In the Tanakh, the equivalent phrase for antichrist is *Mashiach tachat* or the anti-Messiah. The word *tachat* means instead of or under. [52]

---

https://www.wildbranch.org/teachings/word-studies/52anti

In 1st, John 4, the apostle warns the assembly about the spirit of antichrist:

> And every spirit that does not confess Jesus is not from God. This is the spirit of the antichrist, which you have heard is coming and which is already in the world at this time.
>
> −I John 4:3, BSB

It is believed that John the apostle penned this message around 95 AD. He informs the people that antichrist are already among them. It is not that a prophet comes speaking against Yeshua, but that their attention is taken away from the Messiah and placed on a man and man-made doctrine.

Yeshua in the book of Revelation warns of further corruption concerning Balaam in the assembly of Pergamum:

> But I have a few things against you, because you have there some who hold the teaching of Balaam, who kept teaching Balak to put a stumbling block before the sons of Israel, to eat things sacrificed to idols and to commit acts of immorality. "So you also have some who in the same way hold the teaching of the Nicolaitans. Therefore repent; or else I am coming to you quickly, and I will make war against them with the sword of My mouth."
>
> −Revelation 2:14-16, NASB

In Revelation 2, Yeshua names the same sins associated with Jezebel. Balaam "had a doctrine" according to Revelation 2:14. In II Peter 2:15: there is a "way of Balaam" that is corrupt and married to the world and the things of the world. Balaam is willing to sacrifice eternal glory for temporary gain and wealth.

The sins of Balaam still exist today. He is mentioned with Cain, who killed his brother over anger and jealousy. Balaam is mentioned with Korah who tried to usurp Aaron and Moses and did not honor the position he already had been given in leadership. "Woe unto them! for they have gone in the way of Cain, and ran greedily after the error of Balaam for reward, and perished in the gainsaying of Core [Korah]" (Jude 1:11 (KJV). Balaam was greedy for gain. Balaam was enticed to please man and not God. In Numbers 22, the king requested Balaam to place a curse on God's chosen people. Possibly, being the chosen soothsayer made him feel important. Hierarchy needed a soothsayer. Balaam, the diviner, would come to the rescue. Could it be that Balaam loved the praises of men too much? He feared man more than the Creator of all. The fear of man always brings a snare. We must be mindful of Balaam, for he resides among us or possibly in us unawares.

Wolves unseen desire wealth, walk in arrogance, and flatter men in order to gain wealth. Pergamum was surrounded by idols. Yeshua knew that His Bride in Pergamum were living in the worst conditions among tyrant narcissistic rulership, but He still brings a word of correction to some there in the community of believers. Some in Pergamum hold to the teachings of Balaam and the Nicolaitans. May it never be us!

Chapter 9

THE TITHE
PART 1

Once while attending a local assembly, I became utterly shocked at the words I heard coming out of the pastor's mouth. I usually agreed with his teachings and found him to be a man who loved the Father, but I was not in agreement with him on this particular topic.

It seems a wealthy couple in the church had opened their home to the youth for a night of fun and activities, and the evening featured a sleepover, hayride, bonfire, and a pizza party at their home. The pastor decided to drop by and say hello to the youth. The following day from behind the pulpit, the pastor described the magnitude of the home and all the extras it had to offer, including a built-in swimming pool. He then loudly exclaimed, "Well, I know who the biggest tithers in my church are! You should have seen the nice big home the [insert names] have! Woo wee," he grinned and talked about testing Adonai in this area. The woman beside me sucked in air and moved uncomfortably in her seat. Her daughters held their crumpled tithe envelopes filled with change and smiled up at me. I knew they were experiencing tough times, eviction even. The pastor spoke on and on about the tithe and prosperity; then, the congregation lined up like good sheep to drop their money into the wooden chest that sat atop the table.

In Mark 12, Yeshua used a widow as an example who gave two small coins to point out the piousness of the Pharisees. And Yeshua said the widow gave more than the chief contributors because she gave out of her poverty:

> As Jesus was sitting opposite the treasury, He watched the crowd putting money into it. And many rich people put in large amounts. Then one poor widow came and put in two small copper coins, which amounted to a small fraction of a denarius. Jesus called His disciples to Him and said, "Truly I tell you, this poor widow has put more than all the others into the treasury. For they all contributed out of their surplus, but she out of her poverty has put in all she had to live on."

> –Mark 12:41-44, BSB

Pastors usually have collections for the tithe, building funds, missionaries, and offerings. Some churches pay a 10% tithe out of their complete collection of tithes to send missionaries out. Some missionaries receive a tithe from the poverty-stricken places they attend and use the seedtime and harvest sermon in their defense. They say to the poor, "I am not going to steal your blessing!" However, throughout the books of the prophets and the New Testament, we are told to care for the poor, widows, orphans, and those in need. Isaiah 58 states that after we share our bread with the hungry, and bring the poor and homeless into our homes and clothe the naked, and take care of our own families, Adonai says that then our light will burst forth:

> Then your light will break forth like the dawn, and your healing will come quickly.
>
> Your righteousness will go before you, and the glory of the LORD will be your rear guard. Then you will call, and the LORD will answer; you will cry out, and He will say, 'Here I am.'"

> –Isaiah 58:8-9, BSB

One of the worst tactics used to influence sheep to give money seems to bring guilt and condemnation and pronounce a curse over the people. I have heard this multiple times while sitting in different congregations, "You all are under a curse and let me tell you why! It's because you have robbed God." Everyone shifts uncomfortably, and then the pastor or elder speaks again, "There is only one place in the Bible where God says, test me in this, and that's the tithe." These pastors use a scripture found in the Book of Malachi to pronounce the curse:

> Will a man rob God? Yet you are robbing Me! But you say, "How have we robbed You?" In tithes and offerings. "You

165

are cursed with a curse, for you are robbing Me, the whole nation of you! Bring the whole tithe into the storehouse, so that there may be food in My house, and test Me now in this," says the LORD of hosts, "if I will not open for you the windows of heaven and pour out for you a blessing until it overflows.

−Malachi 3:8-10, NASB

Pastors will also refer to the "storehouse" mentioned as the church house where they are shepherding. The storehouse/temple was a tithe for the Levitical priests and those who ministered in the temple, and it was food. Food was currency even to the Roman Army and the Samurai, but if it were too far to travel it could be traded for money which was rare but easier to transport−not a lot of mints to make the actual coins. A key point used by pastors refers to the Holy One saying "test me" in this. Often, during the tithe message, a minister will refer to testing God. Some proclaim this is the only time in scripture that we are told of a test concerning Adonai. The Torah says: "You shall not put the Lord your God to the test, as you tested him at Massah" (Deuteronomy 6:16, ESV). The Hebrew words for *test* or *testing* have different meanings. In Deuteronomy 6:16, the word *test* means *try* or *tempt*. It is the word (tə·*nas*·sū) in Hebrew. This word is only found in Deuteronomy 6:16. It is Strong's Hebrew 5254: meaning *to test, try, prove, tempt, assay, put to the proof,* or *test*. Malachi has a different word translated as *test*. In Malachi *test* is the Hebrew word (ū·ḇə·ḥā·nū·nî). It is Strong's Hebrew 974: and it means *to examine, try, prove*. In Malachi, 3, Adonai is not asking to be put to the test. The English translations suggest this in error. The Holy One wants each individual to keep the commandments and examine their hearts. Those Malachi addressed were not following the instructions. They were presenting the Holy One with blind and sick animals and keeping the best for themselves. The Father tells them that it is due to these blind and diseased animals that they do not have favor or blessing. The *test* He presents is for them to keep the commandments in the true spirit of the commandment. Then they will see His rewards for obedience:

> Bring the whole tithe into the storehouse. Then there will be food in My House. Now test Me in this"—says *Adonai-Tzva'ot*—"if I will not open for you the windows of heaven, and pour out blessing for you, until no one is without enough. I will rebuke the devouring pest for you, so it will not destroy the fruit of your land, nor will your vine be barren in the field," *Adonai-Tzva'ot* says. "All the nations will call you blessed. For you will be a land of delight," says *Adonai-Tzva'ot*.
>
> –Malachi 3:10-12, TLV

This formula still works today even without a temple. If we tithe and bring our gifts before the Holy One, He will bless it, but this blessing doesn't always come in the form of money.

The first recorded message of "tithing" is in Genesis 14. Abram gave a tenth of the loot taken from five conquered kings. Abram gives the possessions to Melchizedek, king of Salem (Jerusalem), a priest of Adonai:

> And Melchizedek king of Salem brought out bread and wine. (He was priest of God Most High.) And he blessed him and said, "Blessed be Abram by God Most High, Possessor of heaven and earth; and blessed be God Most High, who has delivered your enemies into your hand!" And Abram gave him a tenth of everything.
>
> –Genesis 14:17-20, ESV

Notice, Abram takes nothing for himself. Abram, later known as Abraham, received tithe from plundering those who had kidnapped his kinsman:

> When Abram heard that his kinsman had been taken captive, he led forth his trained men, born in his house, 318 of them, and went in pursuit as far as Dan. And he divided his forces against them by night, he and his servants, and defeated them and pursued them to Hobah, north of Damascus. Then he brought back all the possessions, and also brought back his kinsman Lot with his possessions, and the women and the people.
>
> –Genesis 14:14-16, ESV

Abram gave ten percent to Melchizedek, and the rest he gave away also. Did Adonai command Abram to tithe? The text does not seem to imply that. Abraham also freed the slaves instead of accepting them from the pagan kings who led the cities Abraham saved.

Later, the topic of tithing is brought up by Jacob. Jacob set out to Haran and stopped for the night, resting his head on a stone. He dreamt of a stairway to heaven with angels descending and ascending on it. Adonai spoke to him about all the blessings He would bestow upon him and that his descendants would be like the dust of the earth. Then Jacob awoke and said:

> If God will be with me and will keep me on this journey that I take, and will give me food to eat and garments to wear, and I return to my father's house in safety, then the LORD will be my God. "This stone, which I have set up as a pillar, will be God's house, and of all that You give me I will surely give a tenth to You.
>
> –Genesis 28:20-22, NASB

Here is a most contradictory conclusion because Jacob did not tithe ten percent and then wait for Adonai to bless him. Instead, Jacob said if Adonai gave him direction, protection, food, and clothing on his journey, then he would give Him a tenth of everything.

The Israelites were an agricultural society. The tithe was given every year, except in the third year, and no tithes were given in the sabbatical year or the 7th year. *The Jewish Encyclopedia* on tithing written by Joseph Jacobs and M. Seligsohn, and Wilhelm Bacher explain this further in *The TITHE:*

> It is to be concluded that, the seventh year being a Sabbatical year and no tithing being permissible therein, the tithe of the first, second, fourth, and fifth years of every cycle of seven years had to be brought to the Temple and eaten by the landowner and his family, while the tithe of the third and sixth years was to be left at home for the poor.

> The third year was called the year of tithing; and after the distribution of the tithe among the Levites and others, the landowners were required to announce solemnly before the Lord that they had observed all the laws connected therewith, concluding such declaration with a prayer for God's blessing (*ib.* xxvi. 12-15). A mourner was not allowed to eat the tithe, nor might one employ it for any unclean use, nor give it for the dead. [53]

Tithing, firstfruits, and offerings are needed, but some pastors are not handling this today with integrity. What is the tithe? In biblical days, tithing was a Torah requirement in which

---

[53] TITHE - JewishEncyclopedia.com

the Israelites were to give a percentage of the crops they grew and the livestock they raised to the tabernacle/temple:

> Every tithe of the land, whether of the seed of the land or of the fruit of the trees, is the Lord's; it is holy to the Lord. If a man wishes to redeem some of his tithes, he shall add a fifth to it. And every tithe of herds and flocks, every tenth animal of all that pass under the herdsman's staff, shall be holy to the Lord.
>
> —Leviticus 27:30-33, ESV

All the other 11 tribes, but the Tribe of Levi who were set apart to serve Adonai, received an inheritance of land/ territory. The Holy One commanded food to be brought into a storehouse as an inheritance for His priests, the sons of Levi:

> To the sons of Levi, behold, I have given all the tithe in Israel for an inheritance, in return for their service which they perform, the service of the tent of meeting. so that the people of Israel do not come near the tent of meeting, lest they bear sin and die.
>
> —Numbers 18:21-22, NASB

> At that time the LORD set apart the tribe of Levi to carry the ark of the covenant of the LORD, to stand before the LORD to serve Him, and to pronounce blessings in His name, as they do to this day. That is why Levi has no

portion or inheritance among his brothers; the LORD is his inheritance, as the LORD your God promised him.

–Deuteronomy 10:6-9, BSB

The sons of Levi also were to give 10% of the tithe given to them unto the Lord:

And the LORD spoke to Moses, saying, "Moreover, you shall speak and say to the Levites, 'When you take from the people of Israel the tithe that I have given you from them for your inheritance, then you shall present a contribution from it to the LORD, a tithe of the tithe.'"

–Numbers 18:25-26, ESV

The people mentioned in Malachi were under a curse because Adonai's chosen priests, those who were to honor Him and care for the sacrifices, were offering Adonai blind, sick animals. Why were they doing this? They were keeping the best for themselves. "But if an animal has a defect, is lame or blind, or has any serious flaw, you must not sacrifice it to the LORD your God" (Deuteronomy 15:21, BSB). The Lord gives a very stern message through the mouth of His prophet Malachi concerning this, but usually when this passage is taught, the whole chapter is not read, and the message is taken out of context:

A son honors his father, and a servant his master. Then if I am a father, where is My honor? And if I am a master, where is My respect?' says the LORD of armies to you, the priests who despise My name! But you say, "How have we despised Your name?" You are presenting defiled food upon My altar. But you say, "How have we defiled You?" In that you say, "The table of the LORD is to be despised." And when you present a blind animal for sacrifice, is it not evil? Or when you present a lame or sick animal, is it not evil? So, offer it to your governor! Would he be pleased with you, or would he receive you kindly?" says the LORD of armies.

–Malachi 1:6-8, NASB

Our offerings unto the Holy One should be the best in everything we do. Our Messiah was the ultimate offering, and he was without spot or blemish. Yeshua Messiah was referred to as the Lamb of God. He was spotless and without blemish. Rabbi Shlomo Yitzchaki (Rashi), an outstanding Biblical commentator of the Middle Ages, explains more about the tithe of the flock:

When he is about to tithe them, he passes them through a door, one after another, and the tenth he strikes with a rod smeared with red dye so that afterwards it should be recognized as one of the tithe. Thus he does to the young sheep and to the calves of each separate year. (Bekhorot 58B) [54]

---

[54] Rashi on Leviticus 27:32:2 with Connections & Bekhorot 58b:10 (sefaria.org)

This red dye represents the blood of Yeshua. The blood on the doorpost in Egypt marked their homes. The angel of death passed over those with the blood marking on the doorpost. Notice the tenth animal and the tenth plague of Egypt and how they correlate. Yeshua is the door to the sheep, and He overcame death and the grave:

> For every tenth part of herd or flock, whatever passes under the rod, the tenth one shall be holy to the LORD. He is not to be concerned whether it is good or bad, nor shall he exchange it; or if he does exchange it, then both it and its substitute shall become holy. It shall not be redeemed.
>
> —Leviticus 27:32-33, NASB

The practice of tithing first appears in the Torah, by Abraham and Jacob but not as a commandment. After the rebellion of Korah (Numbers 16), tithing was instituted by the Holy One. The tribe of Levi did not receive a portion of the Land of Israel. The tithe would support them as they worked in the Tabernacle or the Temple. The Levites would receive the best of the fresh oil, fresh wine, grain, the first fruits. The Levite would then take a tenth of what he received and give it to the kohen (High Priest):

> Then the LORD spoke to Moses, saying, "Moreover, you shall speak to the Levites and say to them, 'When you take from the sons of Israel the tithe which I have given you

from them for your inheritance, then you shall present an offering from it to the LORD, a tithe of the tithe. Your offering shall be credited to you like the grain from the threshing floor or the full produce from the wine vat. So you shall also present an offering to the LORD from all your tithes, which you receive from the sons of Israel; and from it you shall give the LORD'S offering to Aaron the priest.

–Numbers 18:25-28, NASB

Nehemiah gives this same instruction regarding the tithe given to the Levites. After God's people spent 70 years in Babylon, after the first temple's destruction, Nehemiah was given supplies and released as a cupbearer to rebuild the walls of Jerusalem by King Artaxerxes (Darius). Nehemiah was born in Babylon, in exile, but his heart was for his people, and he was instructing the people from the Torah concerning tithes:

And bring to the house of our God the firstborn of our sons and of our cattle, and the firstborn of our herds and our flocks as it is written in the Law, for the priests who are ministering in the house of our God. We will also bring the first of our dough, our contributions, the fruit of every tree, the new wine, and the oil to the priests at the chambers of the house of our God, and the tithe of our ground to the Levites, for the Levites are they who receive the tithes in all the rural towns.

–Nehemiah 10:36–37, NASB

While studying the instructions given in the Torah (Old Testament) concerning the tithe, one must remember the temple is no longer standing, and there is no working priesthood today. Author and Hebrew scholar Dr. Skip Moen breaks down the tithe in a manner that brings it to the 21st century without removing the instructions given in the Torah. In his article titled *Tithe*, Moen asked three questions that need rumination:

Now set aside the exact timing and ask yourself these questions:

1) If the third-year tithe is exclusively for the Levites and the disadvantaged, how can we justify today's collection for buildings, staff, and programs? Aren't we who are followers of the King asked to set aside our third-year tithe exclusively for the poor?

2) If there is no tithe at all in the seventh year, aren't we violating God's explicit orders when we ask (or demand) that every year's offerings go to supporting the "church?"

3) What would happen if we actually tithed according to God's design? Wouldn't we have to change a lot of things that we do under the banner of "church" because we would no longer be pressing the congregation to support

it all? Gee, maybe the "church" would cease operating like a corporation. [55]

The House churches in the Book of Acts seem much less complicated and intimate than dealing with mega-church overhead and, as Dr. Moen stated, operating like a corporation instead of a community. These matters concerning the tithe and offerings can be difficult to weigh in today's world. Giving to the needy, whether they are in another country or family members, is precious in the eyes of the Lord. I cannot travel to India, but my cousin is a missionary there, so when I support her work with the poor there, I, too, am giving. When I support leaders that teach me more about the Messiah and how to walk in a manner pleasing to Him, I am helping them spread the Good News.

---

[55] Tithe | Hebrew Word Study | Skip Moen

THE TITHE
PART 2

When I first learned to hear the Father's voice, I was not always obedient wholeheartedly. Years ago, as I was going through the most painstaking journey of my life and lost everything I owned, one morning, a neighbor phoned. I did not know her that well, but she was close friends with my next-door neighbor, and I had conversed with her a time or two. She asked me if I had recipes for making a cake without eggs. I told her I did not. She opened up that it was her daughter's birthday, and she was out of eggs and did not have enough to make a cake. As she talked, I realized she needed more than eggs. I told her I had everything she needed to make her daughter a cake, but she said she could not allow me to do that. She knew I had been going through difficult times. After hanging up the phone, the Father pressed me to take her groceries. I opened the pantry, took out a cake mix, icing, and oil, and grabbed eggs from the refrigerator but felt pressed that she needed more than dessert. I opened the cabinets and picked out the soups that weren't Campbell's, generic mac-n-cheese, canned goods that I did not like, and items I could do without. Suddenly I heard, "She needs washing powder." I walked into the laundry room and stared at my named brand detergent and an off-brand one that was half full and grabbed the off-brand one.

Feeling good about myself, I loaded the items in my car, drove down the street and around the corner, and knocked on her door. She was in tears. Her two young daughters stood on the porch smiling at me. Suddenly I heard in my spirit that she needed gas money. "Give her the twenty dollars in your pocket," which was a large amount for me since becoming too sick to work or finish my degree. I had already gone through my savings and checking, and my home had gone into foreclosure. My husband had left the country when I was too sick to walk, but I was obedient. I pulled out the twenty-dollar bill and handed it to her.

"This is for gas," I said.

"How did you know I needed gas," she asked, then hugged me and said her car was about empty.

Feeling good in my soul that God had used me to help someone else in need, I drove back home and lay back down to rest as I was still very fatigued. Suddenly I was overcome with conviction. It was as if the Father was telling me, "You did not give her your best. You gave her your second best, your off-brands and generic labels. Do you not trust me to take care of you?" I meditated on my actions and the fact that my heavenly

Father gave His best, His Son, Yeshua. I pulled my exhausted self-off of the couch and went to the store and bought meat and cheese, butter, more eggs, and staple items like peanut butter and oatmeal that would last and left the bags on her porch. In Luke 14 Yeshua gives a most convicting parable concerning the needy:

> Jesus {Yeshua} also went on to say to the one who had invited Him, "When you give a luncheon or a dinner, do not invite your friends or your brothers or your relatives or wealthy neighbors, otherwise they may also invite you in return and that will be your repayment. But when you give a banquet or a reception, invite the poor, the disabled, the lame, and the blind, and you will be blessed because they cannot repay you; for you will be repaid at the resurrection of the righteous (the just, the upright).
>
> –Luke 14:12-14, AMP

On the flip side, in today's world, giving at times has become something some people expect or feel we owe them. Even those holding up signs on the side of the road expect a payout. In 2020 over 10,000 religious organizations took at least 3 billion in coronavirus financial aid from the United States government. According to *The Guardian*, British Daily Newspaper, "The list of recipients of federal Paycheck Protection Program payments includes churches, synagogues, temples and private religious schools. Among them are the ministries of wealthy televangelists accused of fraud and one "secretive sect." [56]

After years of scheming and corruption among the prosperity gospel evangelists, many today shy away from giving. Since the tithe was for the priesthood and was always the produce from the land, some think, "why should I give to this one or that one?" Several ministers, including my husband and me, spend much money behind the scenes. Most social media ministries today have unseen or unnoticed expenses, such as websites, web designers, marketers, editors, book cover designers, zoom business plans, special microphones for podcasts, and video-making. This can be costly. When we enjoy teachings on YouTube or a group lecture online, we must think of the hours behind the scenes spent reading, studying, and putting together slide shows, visuals, marketing, and information packets. Being more aware of gratitude or even thanking the host is a start.

At gatherings many do not help clean up afterwards. Then the ministers get burned out from hosting, planning, cooking, and preparing the lessons. We are to honor leadership. "The elders who lead well are worthy of honor and honorarium— especially those who work hard in the word and teaching" (I Timothy 5:17, TLV). Remember the ten lepers Yeshua healed?

---

[56] Televangelists take a slice as churches accept billions in US coronavirus aid | US news | The Guardian

Only one came back to thank him. ""Were not all ten cleansed?" Jesus asked. "Where then are the other nine? Was no one found except this foreigner to return and give glory to God?" (Luke 17:17-18, BSB).

Giving isn't just money, but at times it is. In I Samuel, the soon-to-be future king, Saul, while looking for his father's donkeys who had escaped, becomes exhausted after several days. Saul's servant suggests he see the prophet Samuel, who will undoubtedly tell him where his father's donkeys have run off to. Saul answers his servant very curiously:

> Then said Saul to his servant, But, behold, if we go, what shall we bring the man? for the bread is spent in our vessels, and there is not a present to bring to the man of God: what have we? And the servant answered Saul again, and said, Behold, I have here at hand the fourth part of a shekel of silver: that will I give to the man of God, to tell us our way. (Before time in Israel, when a man went to inquire of God, thus he spake, Come, and let us go to the seer: for he that is now called a Prophet was beforetime called a Seer.) Then said Saul to his servant, Well said; come, let us go.
>
> —I Samuel 9:7-10, TLV

Saul knew that he could not approach the prophet for information without a gift. Notice, bread would have been a gift. There are so many great places to give gifts today, such as children's hospitals, humane societies, orphanages, helping widows, and so on. There are many ways to give in our communities, such as volunteer at the humane society by walking or shampooing dogs for a day; visit a nursing home or cancer center for children; or help at a homeless shelter. Don't have the time or health to volunteer? Deliver toiletries, toys, pet needs. Most of these places have a list online of things they are in dire need of. Often, when in tune with our Heavenly Father, we give to people who can never repay us, or we give to those who, in return, give to us their words of encouragement, love, time, a listening ear, and a heart full of empathy. Remember Saul would have brought bread to Samuel the prophet, but they had eaten it on their journey.

Ancient Israel, an agricultural society, primarily used agricultural products for their offerings. Although those attending the feast could exchange their festival tithes from farm products to money (Deuteronomy 14:25), they also brought sacrificial offerings to the Holy One:

> And all the tithe of the land, *whether* of the seed of the land *or* of the fruit of the tree, *is* the Lord's. It *is* holy to the Lord. If a man wants at all to redeem *any* of his tithes, he shall add one-fifth to it.
>
> –Leviticus 27:30-31, NKJ

Whatever an Israelite produced from the land was holy and 10% of that produce was God's including animals, but as Leviticus states above, for example, if a man wanted to keep a prized bull because he did not have many, he would have to give 100 shekels plus 20, the 5th. The tithe mentioned in the Torah is such a layered and complex list that education is needed before pronouncing a curse on those who do not give 10% (Malachi 3:9). Through ignorance or greed, leadership pushes congregants to abide by several passages taken out of context such as (Malachi 3:6-10) a passage which was covered in the previous chapter.

The tithes in the Old Testament (*Tanakh*) were for the Levites and the Levitical priests. This priesthood was determined exclusively by bloodline. Most pastors are not Levites; even if they were, most are homeowners and landowners with salaries. Many pastors are retired and get a retirement pension or work an occupation besides the pastoral one. This does not mean a worker is not worth his pay or assemblies do not need money to care for sheep, but the Levites received a portion of the tithe because they were prohibited from owning any part of the land. The Israelite community took responsibility for the Holy One's priests:

> The Levitical priests—indeed the whole tribe of Levi— shall have no portion or inheritance with Israel. They are to eat the offerings made by fire to the LORD; that is their inheritance. Although they have no inheritance among

their brothers, the LORD is their inheritance, as He promised them.

–Deuteronomy 18:1-2, BSB

In the Book of Nehemiah, the nation was shamed because the priests had to abandon the altar and the Torah schools to go work the fields because the people wouldn't tithe after their time in Babylon.

One tithe described in Deuteronomy 14 concerned Adonai's 7th feast, the feast of Tabernacles or Sukkot. This tithe was for the people. God tells them to spend their money on whatever their soul desires, but they were warned not to neglect the Levite:

> When *Adonai* your God blesses you, then you are to exchange the tithe for silver, bind up the silver in your hand, and go to the place that *Adonai* your God chooses. You may spend the money for whatever your soul desires—cattle, sheep, wine, strong drink, or whatever your soul asks of you. Then you will eat there before *Adonai* your God and rejoice—you and your household. But you are not to neglect the Levite within your gates, for he has no portion or inheritance with you.
>
> –Deuteronomy 14:25-27, TLV

The Feast of Sukkot is a time of celebration and reflection. Exodus 23 goes into detail explaining the tithes including the 7th

year, which was a tithe for the poor, but the Holy One does not stop there, He cares for the animals and the land:

> For six years you are to sow your land and gather the increase. But during the seventh year you are to let it rest and lie fallow, so that the poor among your people may eat. Whatever they leave behind, the animals of the field may eat.
>
> —Exodus 23:10-11, TLV

Continuing in Exodus, we learn more about the firstfruit offerings given three times a year:

> Three times in the year you are to celebrate a festival for Me. You are to observe the Feast of *Matzot [Unleavened Bread].* For seven days you will eat *matzot* as I commanded you, at the time appointed in the month Aviv, for that is when you came out from Egypt. No one is to appear before Me empty-handed. Also you are to observe the Feast of Harvest, the firstfruits of your labors that you sow in the field, as well as the Feast of the Ingathering at the end of the year, when you gather your crops from the field. Three times in the year all your men are to appear before *Adonai Elohim.*
>
> —Exodus 23:14-17, TLV

There are seven feasts listed in Leviticus 23. These are called the Holy One's feasts, not Jewish feasts:

Speak to the people of Israel and say to them, these are the appointed feasts of the LORD that you shall proclaim as holy convocations; they are my appointed feasts.

–Leviticus 23:2, ESV

Three of the feasts were called foot festivals because all the men were commanded to travel to Jerusalem and be in the land on foot during these three feasts which are the feast of Unleavened Bread (Passover/*Unleavened*), Pentecost (*Shavuot*), and Tabernacles (*Sukkot*) Exodus 23:14-17.

The firstfruits offerings were from seven fruits given before the harvest–barley, wheat, figs, grapes, pomegranates, dates, and olives. The spring harvest was barley. Yeshua was resurrected at the beginning of the barley harvest; on the exact day the Israelites were to wave their sheaf offerings. This would have been the first bundle of barley from their fields. Messiah Yeshua was the first fruits. Summer consisted of wheat, figs, grapes, and pomegranates. Early fall had dates and olives. All the feasts and offerings represent our Messiah:

> *Adonai* spoke to Moses saying: "Speak to *Bnei-Yisrael* and tell them: When you have come into the land which I give to you, and reap its harvest, then you are to bring the *omer* of the firstfruits of your harvest to the *kohen*. He is to wave the *omer* before *Adonai*, to be accepted for you. On the morrow after the *Shabbat*, the *kohen* is to wave it. On the day when you wave the

omer you are to offer a male lamb without blemish, one year old, as a burnt offering to *Adonai*. [This was the most valuable livestock outside of a bull.]

–Leviticus 23:10-12, TLV

Paul tells us that Yeshua is our firstfruits offering, and He was and is a spotless Lamb without blemish:

But now Messiah has been raised from the dead, the firstfruits of those who have fallen asleep. For since death came through a man, the resurrection of the dead also has come through a Man. For as in Adam all die, so also in Messiah will all be made alive. But each in its own order: Messiah the firstfruits; then, at His coming, those who belong to Messiah.

–I Corinthians 15:20-23, TLV

Notice, the verse says "at His coming" we who believe and belong to Him will then be resurrected from death. Yeshua gave his life, but he did not stay in the grave, and neither will we. HalleluYah!

Giving from the heart is always practical. Again, congregations or assemblies need money to keep the doors open, send out missionaries, and care for widows, orphans, and people experiencing poverty. In the book of Acts, we read of house churches, or gatherings that were part of a community and not a building. One of the most profound scriptures on giving comes from Yeshua's brother:

> Pure and undefiled religion before our God and Father is this: to care for orphans and widows in their distress, and to keep oneself from being polluted by the world.

> –James 1:27, BSB

The feasts are essential in understanding how to care for those less fortunate and for defining tithes and offerings, but Christianity has thrown out the front of the Book that explains the tithe, and because of this many believers have been swindled, manipulated, and tricked into giving money by wolves' unseen.

There is no comparison when comparing the cost of tithes and offerings against what the Messiah gave us and there is no need to test God—only the need to be obedient. Biblical Charity was often person to person to build relationships and mentorship. Of course, we can present a sickly, blind offering to Him in other ways. If the Father tells us to give to a neighbor in need, and we offer our hand-me-downs, outdated food, and leftovers, we, too, will be held accountable. Nature abhors a vacuum; what we give comes back in one way or the other. We are to give our best. A quote from *The Diary of a Young Girl*, by Anne Frank, "No one has ever become poor by giving:"

> Whatever you do, work at it with your whole being, for the Lord and not for men, because you know that you will receive an inheritance from the Lord as your reward.

> –Colossians. 3:23-24 BSB

Chapter 10

TITHING IN THE NEW TESTAMENT

Saint Peter's Basilica was raised over the so-called burial site of the Apostle Peter, who the Catholic Church claimed was the first pope of Rome. Although, more than likely, Peter never even preached in Rome. Peter was called to be an apostle to the Jews. Peter was married according to scripture in I Corinthians 9:5 and Matthew 8:14. Being married does not fit the lifestyle of a Pope. Peter was sent to the lost sheep of the House of Israel. "To the sojourners of the Diaspora in Pontus, Galatia, Cappadocia, Asia, and Bithynia—" (I Peter 1:1, TLV). *The King James Version* uses the term *strangers* in place of sojourners. It was Paul who was sent to the Gentiles, as covered in chapter 2.

Multiple doctrines and corruption have crept into both the Catholic Church and the protestant congregations. The Catholic Church has billions invested in foreign companies and owns more land, properties, cathedrals, monasteries, schools, and convents than one could imagine. Do they help the poor and have great charities? Yes, they do, but they also hoard wealth, as do many Protestant churches who have built kingdoms here as well:

> According to the National Post News, there is no way to count the wealth of the Catholic church. The church has acquired priceless art, gold, the apostolic palace, the Sistine Chapel, and Saint Peter's Basilica, the largest church in the world. [57]

Television ministers have come under the radar of late. Many times, the smiling faced television evangelists who quote scriptures and offer prayers and doctrines that tingle the ears are, in fact, wolves in sheep's clothing. Megan Schmidt, an author at *Beliefnet Christian Community*, exposes the corruption of shepherds and evangelists in her article titled *8 Richest Pastors in America*. One man who had a lot of exposure in the 1990s and early 2000s with his healing lines and sold-out arenas is televangelist Benny Hinn. According to the article, Hinn has a Net Worth of $42 Million. Kenneth Copeland, who leads the "*Believer's Voice of Victory*" TV show and network, is a giant within the Word of Faith branch of Pentecostalism. Kenneth Copeland Ministries operates on a 1,500-acre campus near Fort Worth, TX, equipped with a church, a private airstrip, and a hangar for the ministry's $17.5 million jet and other aircraft. His net worth is 750 million. Creflo Dollar is an

---

[57] https://nationalpost.com/news/wealth-of-roman-catholic-church-impossible-to-calculate

American televangelist, pastor, and the founder of the non-denominational World Changers Church International (WCCI) based in College Park, Georgia. Creflo Dollar's annual salary is estimated to be $4.54 Million. [58]

The Bible is full of warnings about money and power. Possessions in the book of Acts showcases a people who were of one mind and one heart:

> Fear lay upon every soul, and many wonders and signs were happening through the emissaries. And all who believed were together, having everything in common. They began selling their property and possessions and sharing them with all, as any had need. Day by day they continued with one mind, spending time at the Temple and breaking bread from house to house. They were sharing meals with gladness and sincerity of heart, praising God and having favor with all the people. And every day the Lord was adding to their number those being saved.
>
> –Acts 2:43-47, TLV

What did the apostles do with the money? Did they hoard it or spend it on luxurious items? According to scripture they did just the opposite:

---

[58] 8 Richest Pastors in America | Net Worth Joel Osteen, Pat Robertson, Kenneth Copeland | Pastor's Salaries - Beliefnet

Now the whole group of those who believed was one in heart and mind. No one would say anything he owned was his own, but they had everything in common. With great power the emissaries were giving witness to the resurrection of the Lord *Yeshua,* and abundant favor was upon them all. No one among them was needy, for all who were owners of lands or houses would sell them and bring the proceeds and set them at the feet of the emissaries. And the proceeds were distributed according to the need each one had.

–Acts 4:32-35, TLV

When a community is one, and of one heart and mind, the shepherds care for the flock, the poor, widowed, or sick. It is a community of righteousness. This looks very different from the corruption that has crept into the "church."

Paying tithes is not a hocus-pocus path to wealth and riches. It is not a lottery ticket to becoming famous and obtaining a mansion. Those who are a part of this corrupt gospel often give all the glory to the Father for their worldly wealth. Giving is not a gimmick where we place ten percent in the offering plate and wait for checks to arrive in the mail. There are some congregations where the shepherds have the people stand and make declarations over their money for wealth. Here is one proclamation repeated every week and televised at a local congregation:

I fully expect unexpected income now. I will receive newfound monies and checks in the mail. I receive an increase of prosperity now. I am a recipient of the transference of the wealth of the wicked. I will have no more oppression, no more harassment. I have supernatural protection from heaven, and all of my debts are removed. I am free from debt. Right now and forevermore. I (we) command the angels of God, go now, and bring to pass what I (we) have confessed. [59]

Where does the Holy One in scripture tell us to speak declarations over our money? This doctrine stems from Gnosticism and the belief that we are "little gods"; therefore, we can basically speak things into existence/cast spells or have God's authority without his character.

Did Paul or Peter collect money and brag about the wealth they had accumulated? Did they hold up their huge money bags and proclaim, "To God be the glory!" No, they collected the money for the poor. The pompousness of thinking a person can command a Heavenly Being as the prayer above states is beyond scope. When Samson's father asked the angel his name, he said it was too wonderful and beyond his understanding to even ask such a question (Judges 13:18), but according to these the false prophets, we are to command angels to bring us wealth. Do we have the power to command angels to go and come? This is a

---

[59] Books – Bob Rodgers Ministries

pride matter. Adonai commands angels and sends them; we don't. Furthermore, this is a stench in His nostrils: "Yet in the same way these dreamers defile their bodies, reject authority, and slander glorious beings" (Jude 1:8, BSB).

The Holy One is the only one who commands and sends forth His messengers/angels. This walk is not about us or our lifestyle being cushy and prosperous; it's about standing firm until the end. "But the one who perseveres to the end will be saved" (Matthew 24:13, BSB). It's about helping the helpless and those who can never repay us. Paul has much to say in the book of Titus about false teachers and money: "They must be silenced because they are turning whole families away from the truth by their false teaching. And they do it only for money" (Titus 1:11, NLT). I know widows on disability who give their money to evangelists who make over six hundred thousand a year and live in multi-million-dollar homes. This is terrible. Paul said:

> For if I do this voluntarily, I have a reward; but if against my will, I have stewardship entrusted to me. What then is my reward? That, when I preach the gospel, I may offer the gospel without charge, so as not to make full use of my right in the gospel.
>
> –I Corinthians 9:17-18, NASB

Still, many Christian leaders do not take a salary but live off the sale of books, real estate, and other financial means. Other

Christian leaders give much towards the ministry and live humbly.

Tithing precepts originated in the Torah, which many today refer to as the law. Interestingly, many ministers do not believe we are under the law, and yet tithing is from the law/Torah. Many will retort, "You can't outgive God," and they preach a system of sowing and reaping to gain wealth.Certain denominations teach that when a person gives money, BAM! – God gives you prosperity. I know many poor people who are givers who have yet to become wealthy financially. Is wealth something Yeshua taught? Yeshua said, "Do not store up for yourselves treasures on earth, where moth and rust destroy, and where thieves break in and steal" (Matthew 6:19, NASB).

Some Christians consider their wealth a testimony to the blessings of God. "When you eat and are satisfied, you are to bless the LORD your God for the good land that He has given you" (Deuteronomy 8:10, BSB). Yes, He will bless us. The Holy One also wants us to be a blessing to the poor, the widow, the fatherless, the homeless, and so forth. Having a fine home filled with nice things is not a sin. "There is precious treasure and oil in the home of the wise, but a foolish person swallows it up" (Proverbs 21:20. NASB). What is treasure and oil in a house? The wise virgins had extra oil for their lamps. Oil is a representation of the Holy Spirit and the anointing. Our bodies are the temple of the Holy Spirit. In Psalms 119, the Torah is defined as a treasure worth more than gold. Proverbs 21 is speaking of the Torah as a treasure. "Thy word I have treasured in my heart, that I may not sin against thee" (Psalm 119:11, KJV). In Matthew 6, Yeshua plainly says that where a person's treasure is, there their heart will be also.

Yeshua warned of practicing our righteousness before men to be seen by them, and he called out those who announced their giving with great pomp in the temple courts. The inner area of the Temple had three courts. The easternmost court was the women's court, and it contained the Temple treasury where people donated their money. There were thirteen chests in the court of the women called *Shopheroth*. This Hebrew word is translated in the Bible as a trumpet. The chests were narrow at the bottom and wide at the top, similar to an oil funnel:

> So when you give to the poor, do not sound a trumpet before you, as the hypocrites do in the synagogues and in the streets, so that they may be honored by men. Truly I say to you, they have their reward in full.
>
> –Matthew 6:2, KJV

Imagine Yeshua standing by, watching the spectacle of money being placed in these *shoperoths*. He sees those who look around for the High priest and the Pharisees and then slam their coins in, making a loud trumpet sound. Everyone hears their loud clanging. Along comes a little widow, and Yeshua sees her put her two mites in. Her coins (*prutahs*) barely make an audible ding. The widow's coins make no loud sound if any at all. She was the perfect example for the Master to use. The wealthy men in charge of the storehouse divvied out to those they held in esteem. It was a corrupt system. The rich became richer, and the poor became poorer. Right before the widow walks up to drop her coins in, Yeshua says this:

> "Watch out for the *Torah* scholars, who like to walk around in long robes. They like greetings in the marketplaces, the best seats in the synagogues, and places of honor at feasts. They devour widows' houses and make long prayers as a show. These men will receive greater condemnation!"

> –Mark 12:38-40, TLV

Yeshua explains clearly that they are the ones taking money from the widows.

According to Bible history, there was a special treasury chamber. This chamber was where devout persons secretly deposited money for education and the impoverished children. There was also what was called a *chamber of the silent*:

> Trumpets 9, 10, 11, 12, and 13 were destined for what was left over from trespass-offerings, offerings of birds, the offering of the Nazarite, of the cleansed leper, and voluntary offerings. In all probability this space where the thirteen Trumpets were placed was the "treasury," where Jesus taught on that memorable Feast of Tabernacles

(John 7 and 8; see especially 8:20). We can also understand how, from the peculiar and known destination of each of these thirteen "trumpets," the Lord could distinguish the contributions of the rich who cast in "of their abundance" from that of the poor widow who of her "penury" had given "all the living" that she had (Mark 12:41; Luke 21:1). But there was also a special treasury-chamber, into which at certain times they carried the contents of the thirteen chests; and, besides, what was called "a chamber of the silent," where devout persons secretly deposited money, afterwards secretly employed for educating children of the pious poor. [60]

Paul said, "Each one must do just as he has purposed in his heart, not grudgingly or under compulsion, for God loves a cheerful giver" (II Corinthians 9:7, NASB). He loves a joyful giver, and also a silent one, one who does not make loud trumpet sounds.

In Acts 11, we learn that prophets were still operating fully, and one named Agabus warned of a global famine. They gathered money for their brothers and sisters in Judea. This is how a body of believers operates:

Now at this time some prophets came down from Jerusalem to Antioch. One of them, named Agabus, stood up and indicated by the Spirit that there would definitely

---

[60] https://www.bible-history.com/court-of-women/the_temple_treasury.html

be a severe famine all over the world. And this took place in the reign of Claudius. And to the extent that any of the disciples had means, each of them determined to send a contribution for the relief of the brothers and sisters living in Judea. And they did this, sending it with Barnabas and Saul (*Sha'ul*) to the elders.

–Acts 11:27-30, NASB

Instead of stockpiling rice and beans and ammunition to keep other believers away from the table, they built a bigger table. Paul, Agabus, and Barnabas were active in stirring up the believers to this work of compassion. Paul and the disciples delivered money to the needy. The money was not used to purchase crushed velvet pews, golden chairs, or produce amazing stage shows to entertain the crowds. Paul did not hoard money and use it for his pleasure. It was for the poor and the community:

Now concerning the collection for the saints, as I directed the churches of Galatia, so do you also. On the first day of every week each one of you is to put aside and save, as he may prosper, so that no collections be made when I come. When I arrive, whomever you may approve, I will send them with letters to carry your gift to Jerusalem; and if it is fitting for me to go also, they will go with me.

–I Corinthians 16:1-3, NASB

If there had been no leaders in Paul's day who were dishonest or used the gospel as a means to receive filthy gain, he would have no need of speaking as he does throughout the New Testament:

> I have coveted no one's silver or gold or clothes. You yourselves know that these hands ministered to my own needs and to the men who were with me. In everything I showed you that by working hard in this manner you must help the weak and remember the words of the Lord Jesus, that He Himself said, "It is more blessed to give than to receive."
>
> –Acts 20:33-35, NASB

It is more blessed to give than receive when we are giving to those in need. Sometimes that giving is our time and words of encouragement. There is nothing more precious to a person in a hospital bed, a nursing home, or prison than our time. Usually, after this type of ministry, we realize we were the ones ministered to. We recognize our own poverty and lack of gratefulness. But sadly, many poor widows are giving to the healthy, wealthy, and able. Today we see the disabled and fixed-income recipients helping men and women live in million-dollar homes and own private jets, while the helpers themselves eat canned tuna. The disciples and apostles were men with an anointing. Most were fishermen. Nevertheless, these men were not living in a gated community or a mansion. Those who have worked hard and built businesses by the sweat of their brow and brains more power to them, but we must remember we will take nothing out of this world. Yeshua said it was harder for a camel to go through the eye of a needle than for a rich man to enter the kingdom of heaven. Why do so many boast of their wealth and give the Father all the glory for it when Yeshua warns time and again that it is hard for a rich man to enter the kingdom of heaven? It is not a sin to have wealth if wealth doesn't have us:

> Do not store up for yourselves treasures on earth, where moth and rust destroy and where thieves break in and steal. But store up for yourselves treasures in heaven, where neither moth nor rust destroys and where thieves do not break in or steal. For where your treasure is, there will your heart be also.
>
> –Matthew 6:19-21, TLV

Can time or service be used as tithe if a person has no money? I believe so. No matter what amount of money a person makes, whether much or little, he or she can still be consumed with money. The Bible tells us plainly that the love of money is the root of all evil:

> For we brought nothing into the world, and we cannot take anything out of the world. But if we have food and clothing, with these we will be content. But those who desire to be rich fall into temptation, into a snare, into many senseless and harmful desires that plunge people

into ruin and destruction. For the love of money is a root of all kinds of evils.

–I Timothy 6:7-10, ESV

What belongs to Adonai? He is Lord over all. When people give to prominent, wealthy ministers living in luxury are they truly giving to Adonai? These ministers profess that they are winning souls, but the Messiah, way before the cross, informed Zacchaeus that salvation had come to his house when he, Zacchaeus, declared he would pay those he had stolen from and give money to the poor:

> So Zacchaeus hurried down and welcomed Him joyfully. And all who saw this began to grumble, saying, "He has gone to be the guest of a sinful man!" But Zacchaeus stood up and said to the Lord, "Look, Lord, half of my possessions I give to the poor, and if I have cheated anyone, I will repay it fourfold." Jesus said to him, "Today salvation has come to this house, because this man too is a son of Abraham. For the Son of Man came to seek and to save the lost.

–Luke 19:6-10, BSB

When the people asked John the Baptist what they could do to be saved, He said give a coat to someone who has none. "John replied, 'Whoever has two tunics should share with him who has none, and whoever has food should do the same'" (Luke 3:11, BSB). John said bring forth good fruit that is worthy of repentance. Many will have to give an account on judgment day for what they did with the tithes and offerings allotted to them. "One who is gracious to a poor man lends to the LORD, and He will repay him for his good deeds" (Proverbs 19:17, NASB).

America has an assembly or church building on every corner. The money spent to house the body of Yeshua weekly could be used for better means if we were not so divided. A multimillion dollar building on every corner, across the corner from other buildings, is often used only 6 hours a week. Cathedrals are open 3 times a day for Mass and 7 days a week for confession. In the model of the Synagogue, the place of worship is also a community center and a school during the day. It's not just open 2 days a week. In the book of Acts, believers gathered in houses. There were no denominations or non-denominations, no division. In Luke 9, Yeshua sends out His disciples with instructions and those instructions speak volumes and are completely opposite of what we see today:

> He [Yeshua] sent them out to proclaim the kingdom of God and to heal. And He said to them, "Take nothing for the journey—no walking stick, no travel bag, no bread, no money, nor even to have two shirts. Whatever house you enter, stay there and depart from there. And whoever does not receive you, when you leave that town, shake off the dust from your feet as a witness against them."
>
> –Luke 9:2-5, TLV

Yeshua says we are to take nothing on the journey when we go forth in obedience to preach or teach the Good News. An honor/shame culture values honor and avoids shame. In an honor/shame culture traveling rabbis and teachers were fed, housed, and clothed by those who heard them—cash was almost non necessary. It would be a disgrace and extreme insult on behalf of the entire town to not do so. We don't have an honor/shame culture though. When my husband and I are travelling to speak or have a book signing, we often have to pay for our hotel rooms, rent a table, put gas in our car, or purchase plane fare and provide for our own meals. Unthinkable to a 1st Century Jew in many ways, especially if those who go forth are students of a famous rabbi the others claim to follow.

Do our coins enter the trumpet and clank loudly, or are we in a secret place with Adonai? I have a question: Where is your treasure? Do you treasure the poor? Here is my closing advice on the matter. May we give and give with joy. May we give out of our poverty. May we give out of our abundance. May we give more than money and be thankful, content even with what Adonai has blessed us with:

> Whoever has two tunics should share with him who has none, and whoever has food should do the same.
>
> —Luke 3:11, BSB

CLOSING

Book Three, *Wolves Unseen,* uncovers false prophets, wolves in sheep's clothing, covert cults, and the prosperity gospel. You are given a glimpse into the roots of Christianity and those who paved the way for the "Church" today with all Her victories and all Her corruption. The church, like Satan, has evolved and become a trillion-dollar empire. The Reverend Richard Halverson, the American Presbyterian minister and author who served as the chaplain of the United States Senate, said it best:

> In the beginning, the church was a fellowship of men and women centering on the living Christ. Then the church moved to Greece, where it became a philosophy. Then it moved to Rome, where it became an institution. Next, it moved to Europe, where it became a culture, and finally, it moved to America, where it became an enterprise. [61]

The word *church* comes from the Greek word *ekklēsía,* meaning an assembly. The same word is used in the Greek Septuagint from Torah to Revelation, but when it is

---

[61] Top 13 RICHARD HALVERSON quotes and sayings (inspiringquotes.us)

suddenly and out of nowhere translated as *Kirche* or *Church*, Germanic place name, it is very confusing and gives the appearance of two different entities—Israel vs Church. The Church is not about a place or building. The Church is not an institution. Yeshua's Body is not about the many titles we have foolishly placed upon it. The true Bride of the Messiah's eyes and ears have been opened to the wolves in sheep's clothing. The Bride has made herself ready. Her garments are being purified, without spots or wrinkles. She has intimacy with her King and something tangible that does not entertain the likes of Balaam, Cain, Korah, or the doctrines and teachings of the Nicolaitans and Jezebel.

Christianity has traveled far from the simple Gospel our Messiah taught on hillsides, from fishing boats, a woman at a well, houses, and even cemeteries. Christianity, with all its mission fields, elaborate church cathedrals, and YouTube platforms, has a vastly different leadership structure and process. Not only has Christianity traveled far from what it looked like in the days of Yeshua, but it has also traveled far from the commandments written in the Book.

Wolves Unseen uses the book of Proverbs as a proof text to uncover the characteristics of the harlot religious system and the true bride of Messiah in drastic juxtaposition.

The harlot cries out in the streets:

> Then a woman came out to meet him, with the attire of a harlot and cunning of heart. She is loud and defiant; her feet do not remain at home. Now in the street, now in the squares, she lurks at every corner.

> –Proverbs 7:10-12, BSB

Wisdom is crying out in the streets:

> Does not wisdom call out, and understanding raise her voice? On the heights overlooking the road, at the crossroads, she takes her stand. Beside the gates to the city, at the entrances, she cries out.

> –Proverbs 8:2-3, BSB

The harlot is loud, defiant, and seductive, but the voice of wisdom offers instructions, knowledge, and understanding worth more than silver or gold. *Wolves Unseen* looks at wisdom in female form and also the many women who were in authority throughout the Bible, and one woman who ranked with Moses, Deborah, who was a judge and a prophetess:

> Now Deborah, a prophetess, the wife of Lapidoth, was judging Israel at that time. And she would sit under the palm tree of Deborah between Ramah and Bethel in the mountains of Ephraim. And the children of Israel came up to her for judgment.

> –Judges 4:4, NKJ

Unmasking the Unseen Series, excavated and dug trenches into territories of which many are unaware. In Book Three, *Wolves Unseen*, we uncovered the fastest-growing religions in America—Satanism and Wicca, as well as the Christian witch movement and why it is progressing among the younger generation and gaining more and more followers.

To pull up a root system and a tree older than time, with all its falseness and debauchery, we Believers must unite and become the Bride of Christ, Messiah Yeshua. We must moisten the soil so that this root system from the tree of Christianity slides out of the ground and is thrown into the fire. The Apostle Paul explains that we were engrafted into a different tree:

> If the firstfruit is holy, so is the whole batch of dough; and if the root is holy, so are the branches. But if some of the branches were broken off and you—being a wild olive— were grafted in among them and became a partaker of the root of the olive tree with its richness, do not boast against the branches. But if you do boast, it is not you who support the root, but the root supports you.
>
> —Romans 11:16-18, TLV

Replacement theology has caused much damage, but so has Judaism. And, further, with so many voices and teachers, it is hard at times to know who has the "truth."

I hope you are enjoying this Four-Part Series, *Unmasking the Unseen*. Book One, *Satan Unmasked*, investigates Satan with a more Hebraic lens, the history of Satan, and how he has evolved. Book Two, *Spirits Unveiled*, delves into all things concerning angelic beings, demonic spirits, witchcraft, sorcery, and deliverance. Book Three, *Wolves Unseen,* examines wolves in sheep's clothing, cults, the tithe, the role of women, and a system that has pulled the wool over the eyes of Christians for centuries. Next, Book Four, *King Revealed*, uncovers who the Messiah is and who He is not. Yeshua, too, has been changed by the church system into a weakened savior who heads up congregations filled with lawlessness and anything-goes mentalities. He has become a *Gnostic Christos*, God made in man's image the way man would have Him to be instead of how He is. How did the Lion from the tribe of Judah become a smiling Savior on a car bumper sticker (Jesus loves you) or a WWJD bracelet (what would Jesus do?)? But will the real Messiah please stand up?

I hope you are enjoying this series and will continue with *King Revealed*.

Blessings,

Tekoa Manning

DON'T GO YET!

Thank you for reading Book Three, *Wolves Unseen*, of the *Unmasking the Unseen Series*. I hope you already enjoyed Book One, *Satan Unmasked*, and Book Two, *Spirits Unveiled*, and continue with Book Four, *King Revealed*. These books have been a labor of love and have taken years of research to complete. Your feedback and thoughts are important to me.

COULD YOU HELP ME?

Please leave me an honest review. It would mean so much to me and the proceeds will help with our financial support to the orphans and widows in India and Malawi.

Please also refer this Book Series, *Unmasking the Unseen*, to those who may benefit from it. For updates and new book releases, go to Tekoamanning.com.

Blessings & Shalom,
Tekoa Manning
Manning the Gate Publishing LLC

SOURCES

1. Smith, Steve, *Broken Cisterns: Cultic Codependency (2-26-2013)* Liberty for Captive website. Retrieved on 8-20-2023. Broken Cisterns: Cultic Codependency (Part 1 of 2) | Liberty for Captives

2. Hogan, Kathleen, *University of Virginia's American Studies hypertext project on Henry Nash Smith's Virgin Land . The Shakers.* (No dates). Retrieved on *6-8-2022. Introduction (virginia.edu)*

3. CBS NEWS, *143 sheep suffocate in pileup while fleeing two wolves in Idaho: "The wolves scared the hell out of" the flock. (6-3-2022).* The Associated Press. Retrieved on 6-8-2022. 143 sheep suffocate in pileup while fleeing two wolves in Idaho: "The wolves scared the hell out of" the flock - CBS News

4. Rich, R. Russell (2d ed. 1967). *Those Who Would Be Leaders: Offshoots of Mormonism* (Provo, Utah: Brigham Young University) *Arnold Potter (1804-1872).* Familypedia. (No date) Retrieved on 6-4-2022. Arnold Potter (1804-1872) | Familypedia | Fandom

5. Slick, Matt, *Mormonism, World Religions.* (12-17-1008). Christian Apologetics and Research Ministry. Retrieved on 6-5-2022. Joseph Smith boasted that he did more than Jesus | carm.org

6. Jansen, Hans, The Global Embassy for Israel, *The Historical Roots of the Anti-Israel Positions of Liberal Protestant Churches. (6-1-2007) Retrieved on 6-17-2022. The Historical Roots of the Anti-Israel Positions of Liberal Protestant*

Churches (jcpa.org)Understanding the freeze/collapse trauma response can improve our response to survivors' stories — Wagatwe Wanjuki

7. Bunyan, John, *The Pilgrim's Progress*, ed. with an introduction by Roger Sharrock Harmondsworth: Penguins Books, 1965) pg. 10. Wikipedia. (No dates given) Retrieved on 5-20-2023. https://en.wikipedia.org/wiki/The_Pilgrim%27s_Progress#cite_note-Sharrock-14

8. Hajdu, Steven, WIRED Science. *Galileo to Turing: The Historical Persecution of Scientists. (6-22-2012) Retrieved on 1-20-2023.* Galileo to Turing: The Historical Persecution of Scientists | WIRED

9. Battell, Patrick Ex-Catholics for Christ, The Catholic Inquisition: "A Medieval Holocaust!" (no date given) Retrieved on 6-27-2023. https://excatholicsforchrist.com/?s=inquisition

10. Howard, Krissy, Edited By Kuroski John. History/Science, Today in History website. *The True Story Of Bloody Mary, The Woman Behind The Mirror* (7- 28- 2022) Retrieved on 3-13-2023. https://allthatsinteresting.com/bloody-mary#:~:

11. Edward, Ryan, A, Britannica Encyclopedia. *Spanish Inquisition Spanish history [1478–1834] (updated 5-8-2023). Retrieved on 5-16-2023. Spanish Inquisition | Definition, History, & Facts | Britannica*

12. Witham, Ted, The Third Order, Society of St Francis. *FRANCISCANS HELPING JEWS IN THE ENGLAND OF HENRY III. (7-21-2013). Retrieved 10-19-2022. Franciscans helping Jews in the England of Henry III | The Third Order, Society of St Francis (tssf.org.au)*

13. *Leasure, Ryan, Ryan* Leasure Blogspot. *Marcion: The Notorious Heretic of the Early Church.* (Published 12- 9-2020) · Updated 12- 31, 2020). Retrieved on 1-23-2023. Marcion: The Notorious Heretic of the Early Church - RYAN LEASURE

14. Krewson, William, Israel My Glory. *The Roots of Replacement Theology. (6-2007). Retrieved on 1-23-2023.* The Roots of Replacement Theology – Israel My Glory

15. Whittaker, Bill, *The Little-Known Purpose of the Cornerstone.* (7-24-2019) Bill Whittaker registered architect design website. Retrieved 6-25-2021. The Little-Known Purpose of the Cornerstone | Blog | Bill Whittaker (billwarch.com)

16. Scott, Brad, WildBranch Ministry, *Anti-christ (2009-2023).* Retrieved on 2-1-2023. Anti-christ — The WildBranch Ministry

17. Moen, Skip, PhD. *Prophet, Priest, Rabbi* (November 21, 2018) Hebrew Word Study. Retrieved on 5-12-2022. Prophet, Priest, Rabbi | Hebrew Word Study | Skip Moen

18. Hoeh, Herman, *WHERE DID THE TWELVE APOSTLES GO?* (No date listed). *NAZARENE NOTES PROCLAIMING THE MESSAGE OF YESHUA THE MESSIAH* Retrieved 8-4-2021. WHERE DID THE TWELVE APOSTLES GO? – NAZARENE NOTES (nazarenesoftheworld.info)

19. Fact Bud, Facts are the Foundation of Truth. *Wolf.* (2013-2023). Retrieved on 10-17-2022. Fun Facts: Wolf - Fact Bud

20. The History Channel. *Witches: Real Origins.* (9- 12-2017) Updated, (10-20-2020) Retrieved (2-22-2019). Witches: Real Origins, Hunts & Trials (history.com)

21. Encyclopedia Almanac. *Magic: Magic In Greco-Roman Antiquity. (No date)* Betz, Hans Dieter, ed. *The Greek Magical Papyri in Translation, Including the Demotic Spells*. 2 vols. Chicago, 1986. (Retrieved on 8-21-2021). Magic: Magic in Greco-Roman Antiquity | Encyclopedia.com

22. Peck-Avery, Alan, *Magic Bowls,* My Jewish Learning website—The Encyclopedia of Judaism. (No dates given) Retrieved on 8-12-2023. https://www.myjewishlearning.com/article/magic-bowls/

23. Yellin, Deena, *'We're in the middle of a witch moment': Hip witchcraft is on the rise in the US. (10-28-2021)*. USA Today. Retrieved 8-2-2022. Witches on the rise in US as TikTok, social media brings it mainstream (usatoday.com)

24. Grant, Hodgson, *Satanic Temple membership explodes as Americans reject politics. (Founder says Trump and Biden are scarier than the devil)*. (10-14-2020) Updated (10-15-2020) The Sun. Retrieved on 1-28-2023. Satanic Temple membership explodes as Americans reject politics & founder says Trump & Biden are scarier than the devil | The US Sun (the-sun.com)

25. The Satanic Temple. *There are Seven FUNDAMENTAL TENETS*. (No date) Retrieved on 11-12-2021. The Satanic Temple - About us - TST

26. Benner, Jeff, A. Ancient Hebrew YouTube Channel. *Did the Serpent in the Bible Lie to the Woman?(2011)*. Retrieved on 12-03-2023. Did the serpent in the garden lie to the woman? - YouTube

27. Animals Network Editors. "*Raven*" Animals.Net (2017). Retrieved on 5-20-2022. Raven - Description, Habitat, Image, Diet, and Interesting Facts (animals.net)

28. Watson, Thomas, Grace Gems Blogsite. *Wise as Serpents—Harmless as Doves.* (No dates given). Retrieved on 5-20-2022. Wise as Serpents (gracegems.org)

29. Animal Corner, *Wolves Fact (No date given) Retrieved on 5-20-2023.* https://animalcorner.org/animals/wolves/

30. Kjorstad, Elise, *(4-26-2021) Science Norway, Wolf packs don't actually have alpha males and alpha females, the idea is based on a misunderstanding. Retrieved on 5-20-2022.*Wolf packs don't actually have alpha males and alpha females, the idea is based on a misunderstanding (sciencenorway.no)

31. Hart, Willa, Grunge. *It Turns Out Alpha Male Wolves Don't Actually Exist In The Wild (8-1-2022). Retrieved on 4-20-2023.* It Turns Out Alpha Male Wolves Don't Actually Exist In The Wild (msn.com)

32. Myatt, Anna, Emmanual Tours. *What is the Valley of Armageddon?* (8-9-2019) Retrieved on 4-19-2022. What is the Valley of Armageddon? | Immanuel Tours (immanuel-tours.com)

33. Psychology Today, (No dates) Retrieved on 6-12-2022. Epigenetics | Psychology Today

34. Abarim Publications. Male Names. *Laban in the Bible*. (No dates given). Retrieved on 4-20-2022. Laban | The amazing name Laban: meaning and etymology (abarim-publications.com)

35. Bowling, Sue Ann, Geophysical Institute. *"Ringstreaked, Speckled, and Spotted"* (9-11- 1987). Retrieved on 4-04-2022. "Ringstreaked, Speckled, and Spotted" | Geophysical Institute (alaska.edu)

36. Benner, Jeff, A, Ancient Hebrew Research Center. *Lord*. (No date given) Retrieved on 11-20-2022. Hebrew Word Definition: Lord | AHRC (ancient-hebrew.org)

37. Benner, Jeff, Ancient Hebrew Research Center. What is Torah? (No date given) Retrieved on 11-12-2023. What is Torah? | AHRC (ancient-hebrew.org)

38. Brown, Michael, L, Ask Doctor Brown. *Why Have Jewish People Been So Hated?* (2- 10- 2009). Retrieved on 11-21-2022. Why Have Jewish People Been So Hated? | Article | AskDrBrown | Your voice for Moral Sanity and Spiritual Clarity | AskDrBrown

39. Safrai, Shmuel, CBE International. Pricilla Papers, The Academic Journal of CBE. (1-21-20020). Retrieved on 7-1-2023. The Place of Women in First-century Synagogues: They were much more active in religious life than they are today - CBE International

40. Freeman, Tzvi, Chabad website, *Why Are There No Female Judges in Torah?* (1-8-2011) retrieved on 8-12-2023. https://www.chabad.org/library/article_cdo/aid/1252255/jewish/Why-Are-There-No-Female-Judges-in-

41. Moen, Skip, Hebrew Word Study. *The Unnamed. (9-1-2019). Retrieved on 12-3-2022.* The Unnamed | Hebrew Word Study | Skip Moen

42. Gallagher, Kisha, *Grace in Torah* website. The Biblical Role of Women Part VII. (5-27-2013). Retrieved on 11-12-2023. The Biblical Role of Women Part VII | GRACE in TORAH

43. Gallagher, Kisha, Grace in Torah website. *Moonbeams and the Moedim Part II* (2-21-2015) Retrieved on 6-12-2023. https://graceintorah.net/2015/02/21/moonbeams-and-the-moedim-part-

44. Mize, Clay, Power of Humility Blogsite. *Lamb of God – The manger in Migdal Eder* (12-25-2014). Retrieved on 12-25-2014. The manger in Migdal Eder literally means the tower of the flock housed the lamb of God just outside Bethlehem. There Jesus the Jewish Messiah was born. (powerofhumility.org)

45. Short, Mike, L. Mayim Hayim Blog site. *Migdal Eder*. (No date given). Retrieved on 12-5-2022. Migdal Eder QRcode generator (mayimhayim.org)

46. Laura & Chaim, Biblical Hebrew Studies, Chaim Ben Torah. *The Gift of the Magi.* (12- 24-2014). Retrieved on 12-5-2022. WORD STUDY – THE GIFT OF THE MAGI | Chaim Bentorah

47. A Place For You. The Revelation of Christ. *Pergamum - The church married to the world. (No date given). Retrieved on 1-8-2023.* Print (aplaceforyou.org)

48. Sheldon, Natasha, History Collection website, *12 Torturous Methods of Execution in History that Will Make You Squirm* (November 15, 2017) Retrieved on 11-20-2022. https://historycollection.com/12-torturous-methods-execution-history/7/

49. Biblical Hermeneutics. *Revelation 2:13 / Satan's earthly headquarter?* (8-21-2018) retrieved on 1-12-2023. Revelation 2:13 / Satan's earthly headquarter? - Biblical Hermeneutics Stack Exchange

50. Keathley, Hampton III, Bible.org. *Studies in Revelation.* (no dates given) retrieved on 1-13-2023. Studies in Revelation | Bible.org

51. Abarim Publication. Male Names. *Balaam in the Bible* (no dates given). Retrieved on 2-1-2023. Balaam | The amazing name Balaam: meaning and etymology (abarim-publications.com)

52. Scott, Brad, WildBranch Ministry, *Anti-christ (2009-2023).* Retrieved on 2-1-2023. Anti-christ — The WildBranch Ministry

53. Jacob, Joseph, Seligsohn, Bacher, Wilhelm, Jewish Encyclopedia. *TITHE* (2002-2021) Retrieved on 3-23-2023. TITHE - JewishEncyclopedia.com

54. Rosenbaum, M, and Silbermann, A.M. London, Seferia. *Rashi on Leviticus 27:32* (1929-1934) Retrieved on 4-2-2023. Rashi on Leviticus 27:32:2 with Connections (sefaria.org)

55. Moen, Skip, Hebrew Word Study, *Tithe*. (7-15-2009) Retrieved on 4-2-2023. Tithe | Hebrew Word Study | Skip Moen

56. Reed, Betsy, The Guardian. *Televangelists take a slice as churches accept billions in US coronavirus aid* (7-9-2020) Retrieved on 5-3-2023. Televangelists take a slice as churches accept billions in US coronavirus aid | US news | The Guardian

57. Morrison, Kristopher, National Post. *Wealth of Roman Catholic Church impossible to calculate* (3-8-2013). Retrieved on 5-3-2023. Roman Catholic Church's wealth impossible to calculate | National Post

58. Schmidt, Megan, Belief net. *8 Richest Pastors in America* (No date given). Retrieved on 5-3-2023. 8 Richest Pastors in America | Net Worth Joel Osteen, Pat Robertson, Kenneth Copeland | Pastor's Salaries - Beliefnet

59. Rodgers, Bob, Evangel World Prayer Center. *Tithing Declaration*. (No dates Given) Retrieved on 5-3-2023. *100*

Days Of Unbroken Prayer and Prayer Guide – Bob Rodgers Ministries

60. Bible History, *The Court of the Women and The Treasury*. (No dates given) Retrieved on 6-1-2023. The Temple Treasury - Bible History (bible-history.com)

61. Inspiring Quotes, *Richard Halverson Quotes and Sayings* (No dates given) Retrieved on 7-1-2023. Top 13 RICHARD HALVERSON quotes and sayings (inspiringquotes.us)